THE FREEDOM CARDS

15 YEARS FIGHTING TO UNDERSTAND FREEDOM

COMPILED AND CURATED BY
ALEX ROBSON

Copyright © 2021 by Alex Robson

All rights reserved. No part of this book may be reproduced or used in any manner without the written permission of the copyright owner except for the use of quotations in a book review. For more information, email: thefreedomcards@gmail.com.

First Edition August 2021

Cover and Layout Design by: The Book Designers

ISBN 978-1-7373254-0-6 (paperback)

www.thefreedomcards.com

To my GIVE West Family...

> Freedom is being able to share our devastating experiences to mitigate future generations from experiencing a similar plight.
>
> Howard Hiroshi Kakita
> Hiroshima A-Bomb Survivor

HOWARD KAKITA
Survivor of the Hiroshima Nuclear Attack

When I was in the 10th grade, I sent 25 letters to politicians and historical figures. I asked them to write their answer to the question, "What does freedom mean to you?" on a 3x5 index card and sign it.

I included a return envelope with my home address and postage. Weeks later, the handwritten cards began to arrive back with messages of unity, challenge, and liberation. Though each card was different, they were connected to the concept of freedom.

I continued sending those requests for the next 15 years.

The cards came back from every corner of the world. As the collection grew, the voices included in the project would vary, coming from different political parties and moral structures. Some were radical, heated, annoyed, and frustrated, while others were happy and positive.

THE FREEDOM CARDS

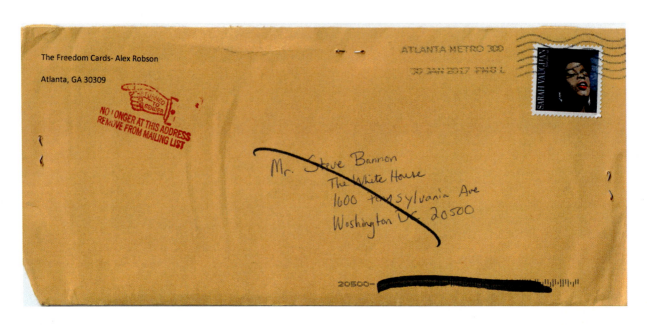

Some letters came back marked "Return to Sender."

THE FREEDOM CARDS

Warren County Historical Society Indianola, Iowa

Freedom is the ability to hope, dream, and pursue life's challenges. Finding the rewards of one's own mind and hands to build a future for yourself and family.

Deborah Taylor
Warren County Historical Society - V.P.
Warren County, Iowa

DEBORAH TAYLOR

Means choices - my right choices - Plans + rights - Peace of mind

Annette Rath

ANNETTE RATH

Freedom means everyone has the right to pursue their talents and interests regardless of income or family background. It also means that the rights of the minority are not overpowered by the majority

Juanita Ott
Retired elementary school teacher

JUANITA OTT

Freedom is living without fear — of physical, mental, or social dangers from a government — based on sex, race, or one's beliefs.

Linda Beatty
Seventy five year old woman living in Iowa most of my life.

LINDA BEATTY

10

In addition to using the mail, I began to collect cards in person, by email, by taking road trips, and through social media. In the summer of 2017, I visited each of the contiguous 48 states to collect Freedom Cards. I met hundreds of amazing people who completed cards, and included their stories in the project.

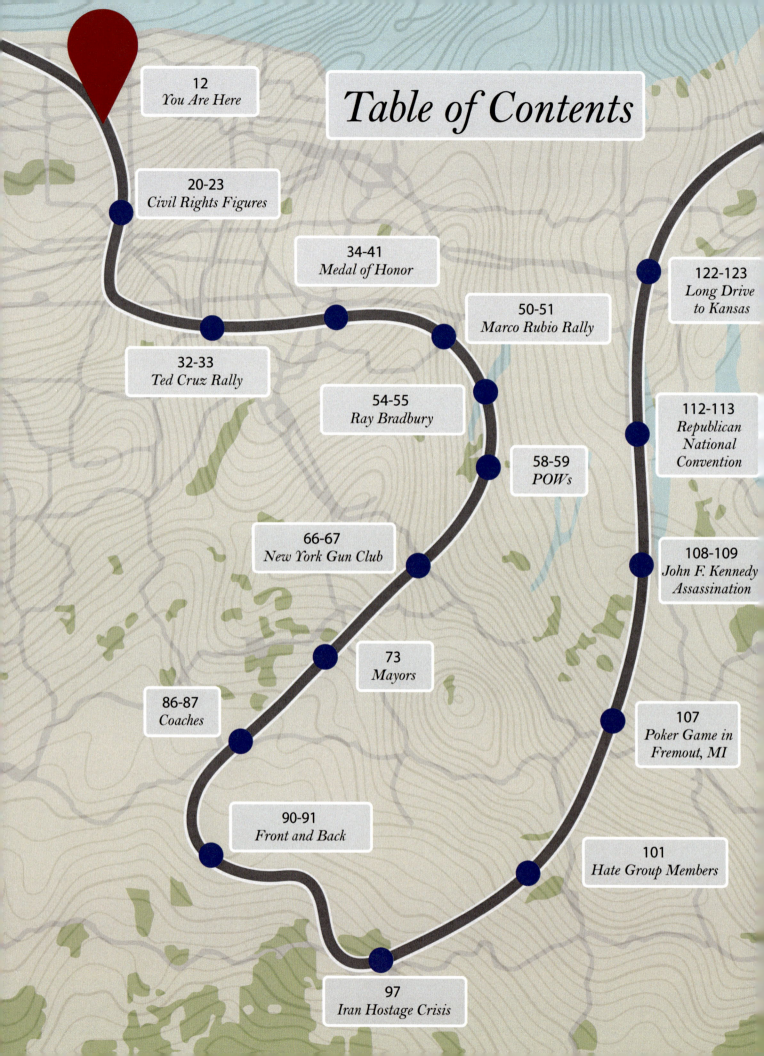

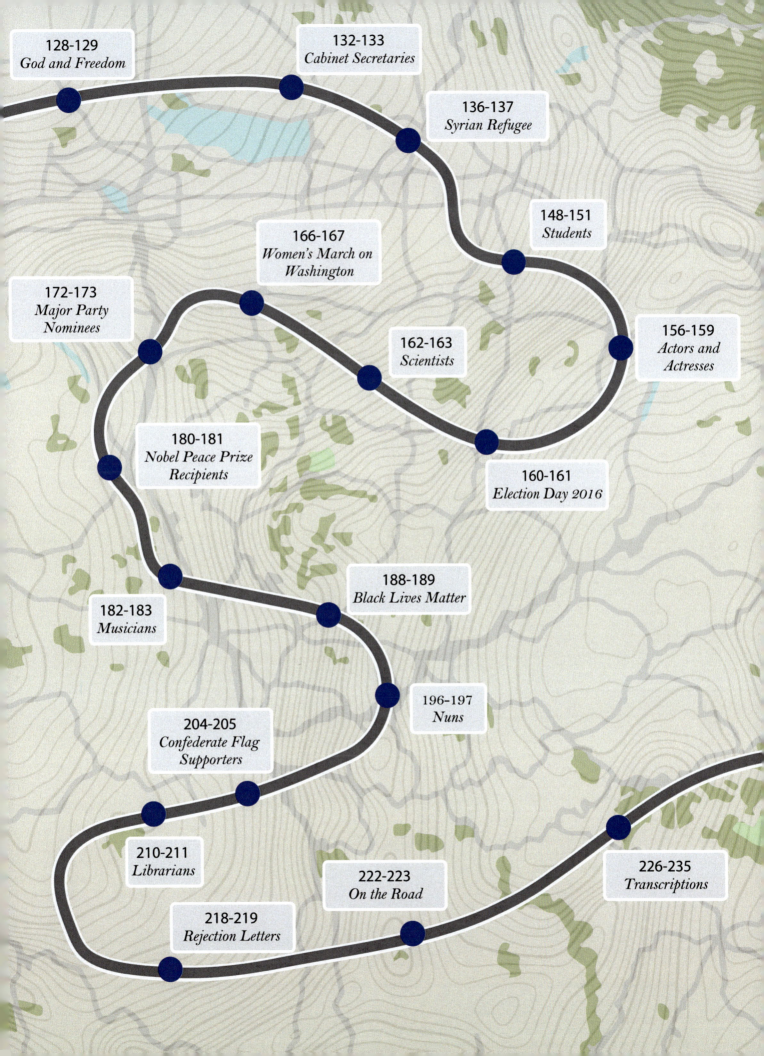

THE FREEDOM CARDS

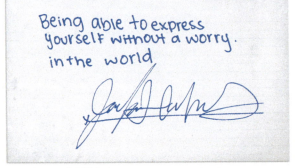

JAYLA, Columbia, South Carolina
Jayla works at a restaurant off of Highway 321.

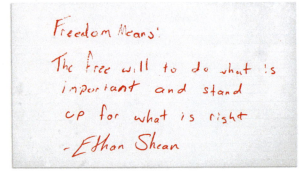

ETHAN SHEAN, Pueblo, Colorado
Ethan works at a marijuana dispensary in Pueblo.

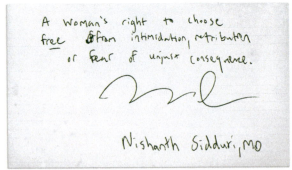

NISHANTH SIDDURI, Philadelphia, Pennsylvania
Nishanth was one of my roommates in college and is now a doctor.

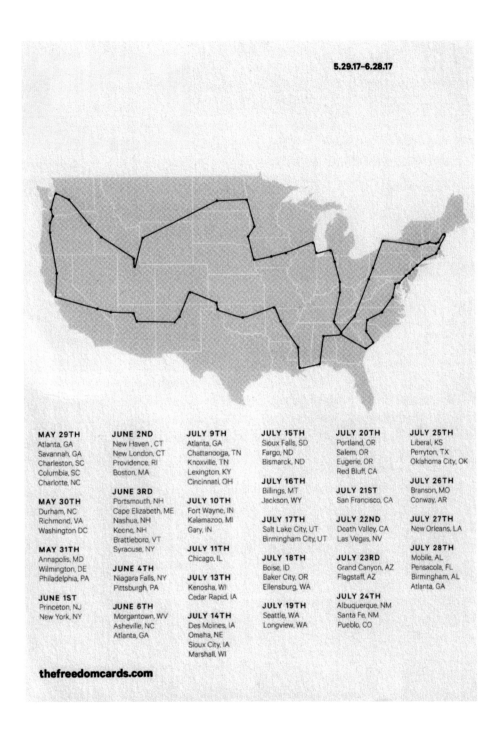

I passed out this postcard while I was driving around the US on The Freedom Road Trip.

THE FREEDOM CARDS

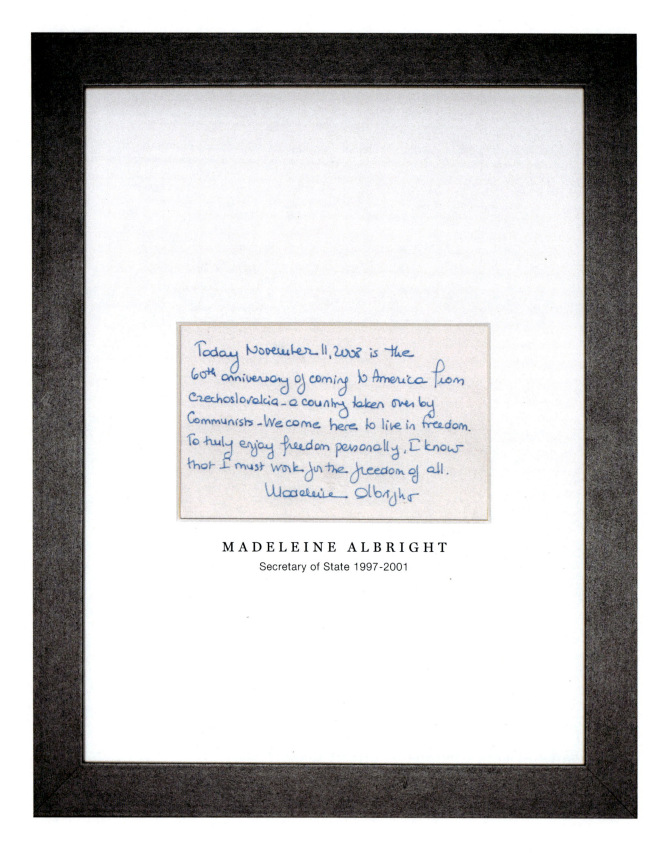

> Today November 11, 2008 is the 60th anniversary of coming to America from Czechoslovakia - a country taken over by Communists - We come here to live in freedom. To truly enjoy freedom personally, I know that I must work for the freedom of all.
>
> Madeleine Albright

MADELEINE ALBRIGHT

Secretary of State 1997-2001

THE FREEDOM CARDS

> Freedom is choosing what we stand for and what we won't stand for and acting accordingly.
> — Jim Mattis, U.S. Marine

GEN. JIM MATTIS
Secretary of Defense 2017-2018

> "Like democracy, freedom is a relatively new concept in history, but the physical experience of freedom is ancient — it means not being confined."
> — Billy Collins, former U.S. Poet Laureate

BILLY COLLINS
Poet Laureate of the United States 2001-2003

> Freedom means to me, being uninhibited by anyone, in reaching one's highest level of productivity and potential in a positive manner.
> — Gloria Gaynor, International recording artist of "I Will Survive" fame.

GLORIA GAYNOR
Musician

> Freedom is such a beautiful thing. One never realizes this, until he has lost it.
> — Everett Alvarez, Vietnam POW – 1964-1973

EVERETT ALVAREZ
Vietnam Veteran, POW

> "Tashi Delek"

REINHOLD MESSNER
Mountain Climber
"Tashi Delek" Tibetan for "Peace and Happiness"

> Freedom means I can be whoever I want to be; say whatever I want to say; believe whatever I want to believe; love whomever I want to love. In other words: It's EVERYTHING.
> — Allison Williams, actress

ALLISON WILLIAMS
Actress

I'm free

very best

CSN

Bush

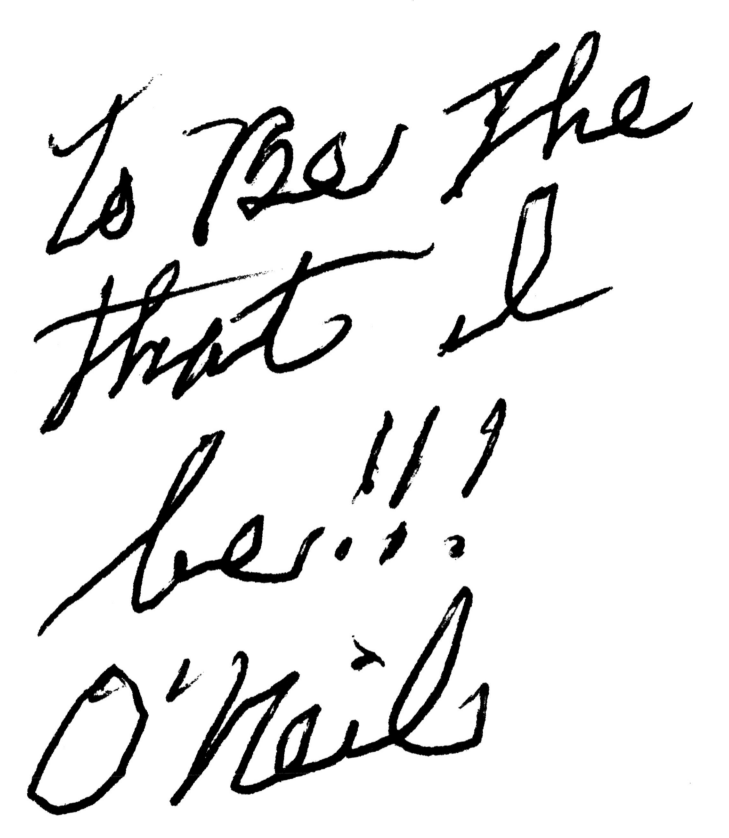

BUCK O'NEIL

Player and Manager in the
American Negro Leagues, d. 2016

THE FREEDOM CARDS

Pennant from The March on Washington for Jobs and Freedom
Collection of the Smithsonian National Museum of African American History and Culture. August 28, 1963

THE FREEDOM CARDS

Freedom means choosing myself and doing as I please in light of taking responsibility for my decisions.

Uriah J. Fields

URIAH FIELDS
Montgomery Bus Boycott

Freedom is a setting in which we can all express the full potential of our god-given possibilities, with mutual respect and acceptance,

Robert S. Graetz — Robert S. Graetz, white minister of black congregation during Montgomery Bus Boycott, and continuing human rights activist through the present.

ROBERT GRAETZ
Lutheran Clergyman and Activist, d.2020

Freedom means Equal and Justice for all.

*Fred D. Gray April 11, 2016
Civil Rights Atty.*

FRED GRAY
Civil Rights Attorney and Activist

Freedom is the human spirit's ability to achieve its highest potential individually and with others.

*Jim Zwerg
'61 Freedom Rider*

JIM ZWERG
1961 Freedom Rider

*12/08/2020 FREEDOM
The legal guarantee and presence of social custom to exercise your right to life, health, opportunities for education, access to meaningful employment, ability to protect your property, your family, and pursue your goals in life without obstacles based on racial or sexual status, religion, or poverty, or barriers imposed on immigration status.*

KATHLEEN CLEAVER
Professor and Member of the Black Panthers

THE FREEDOM CARDS

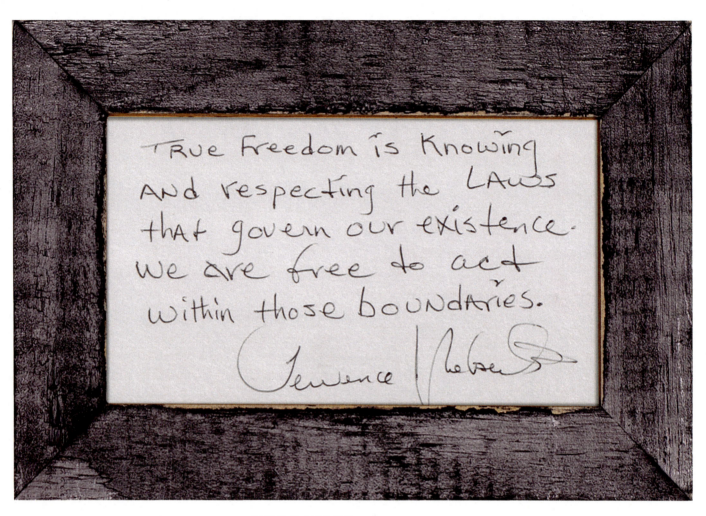

TERRENCE ROBERTS
Little Rock Nine

THE FREEDOM CARDS

RECEIVED OCT - 7 1957
The White House
Washington
CENTRAL FILES

Files
Replies signed by Pres 10/3 and sent to Files 10/4

WA037 NL PD

LITTLE ROCK ARK SEP 30   1957 OCT 1 AM 7 43

THE PRESIDENT
  THE WHITE HOUSE
WE THE PARENTS OF NINE NEGRO CHILDREN ENROLLED AT LITTLE ROCK CENTRAL HIGH SCHOOL WANT YOU TO KNOW THAT YOUR ACTION IN SAFE GUARDING THEIR RIGHTS HAVE STRENGTHENED OUR FAITH IN DEMOCRACY STOP NOW AS NEVER BEFORE WE HAVE AN ABIDING FEELING OF BELONGING AND PURPOSEFULNESS STOP WE BELIEVE THAT FREEDOM AND EQUALITY WITH WHICH ALL MEN ARE ENDOWED AT BIRTH CAN BE MAINTAINED ONLY THROUGH FREEDOM AND EQUALITY OF OPPORTUNITY FOR SELF DEVELOPMENT GROWTH AND PURPOSEFUL CITIZENSHIP STOP WE BELIEVE THAT THE DEGREE TO WHICH PEOPLE EVERYWHERE REALIZE AND ACCEPT THIS CONCEPT WILL DETERMINE IN A LARGE MEASURE AMERICAS TRUE GROWTH AND TRUE GREATNESS STOP YOU HAVE DEMONSTRATED ADMIRABLY TO US THE NATION AND THE WORLD HOW PROFOUNDLY YOU BELIEVE IN THIS CONCEPT STOP FOR THIS WE ARE DEEPLY GRATEFUL AND RESPECTFULLY EXTEND TO YOU OUR HEARTFELT AND LASTING THANKS STOP MAY THE ALMIGHTY AND ALL WISE FATHER OF US ALL BLESS GUIDE AND KEEP YOU ALWASY
  OSCAR ECKFORD JR 4405 WEST 18TH LOTHAIRE S GREEN 1224 WEST 21ST ST JUANITA WALLS 1500 VALENTINE W B BROWN 1117 RINGO LOIS M PATTILLO 1121 CROSS H C RAY 2111 CROSS ELLIS THOMAS 1214 WEST 20TH W L ROBERTS 2301 HOWARD H L MOTHERSHED 1313 CHESTER.

Telegram from the Parents of the Little Rock Nine to President Dwight Eisenhower.
National Archives

THE FREEDOM CARDS

MARTY WALSH
Mayor of Boston, United States Secretary of Labor 2021-

NANCY CHAMBERLAND
Gold-Star Mother

RAY MARSHALL
Secretary of Labor 1977-1981

DONNA SHALALA
Representative, Florida 27th District

MARY WILSON
Vocalist, The Supremes, d.2021

SCOTT ALTMAN
Astronaut, Space Shuttle

KURTWOOD SMITH
Actor

JACK WELCH
Businessman

24

> Freedom for me is living in a country where we wake up to alarm clocks, not bombs, then go and chase our dreams —
>
> Jim Morris

JIM MORRIS
Baseball Player, "The Rookie"

THE FREEDOM CARDS

> Freedom to me is the ability to wake up in the morning and chose how I want to spend my time
>
> Eric Rodriguez

ERIC RODRIGUEZ
Turlock, CA

When on The Freedom Cards Road Trip, I stopped at the Stanislaus County Fair in California. While I was there, a guy named Eric wrote a card, and then his goat ate it.

The Freedom Road Trip
Summer 2017

THE FREEDOM CARDS

> Freedom is the joy to find friendship in this world of whomever we please.
>
> —Frank Pommersheim
> Teacher/Poet

FRANK POMMERSHEIM
Activist, Teacher, Poet

> Freedom: the responsibility to acknowledge & embrace the truth; the obligation to resist the lies of governmental, religious & cultural bigots.
>
> —Nikki Giovanni, Poet

NIKKI GIOVANNI
Poet

> Freedom is our road to happiness —
>
> —Debbie Reynolds

DEBBIE REYNOLDS
Actress, d. 2016

> Freedom means to me the freedom from economic struggle & violence
>
> —Cindy Sheehan
> July 7, 2013

CINDY SHEEHAN
Activist

> FREEDOM BEGETS INNOVATION AND INITIATIVE WHICH BEGETS MORE PROSPERITY, JOY AND HAPPINESS!
>
> —Jeb Bush

JEB BUSH
Governor of Florida 1999-2007

> Freedom is the courage to be fully alive, using every skill, gift, and asset you have to ensure freedom for others.
>
> —Katharine Jefferts Schori
> Presiding Bishop and Primate of The Episcopal Church

KATHARINE JEFFERTS SCHORI
Presiding Bishop of the Episcopal Church 2006-2015

> Freedom is the opportunity to find love, wisdom and happiness wherever we so choose.
>
> —Brandi Chastain
> 3X USA Women's Olympic Soccer Team

BRANDI CHASTAIN
Soccer Player

> Freedom means I make decisions concerning my own life + how I will live it!
>
> —Wes Studi
> '2017'

WES STUDI
Actor

THE FREEDOM CARDS

> Freedom requires responsibility.
>
> — **TOM WATSON**, Professional Golfer

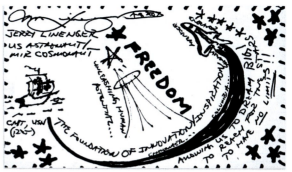

JERRY LINENGER
Astronaut, Space Station Mir, Space Shuttle

> FREEDOM TO ME IS LIVING WITHIN THE AMERICA'S CONSTITUTION. "HOW GREAT IT IS!!"
> 95 YR OLD
> PEARL HARBOR SURVIVOR
> FEB.10.2017
>
> — **ALEX HORANZY**, WWII Veteran, d.2020

> Freedom is having a voice and vote in government.
>
> — **LORETTA SANCHEZ**, Congresswoman, 47th CD
> Representative, California 47th 1997–2017

> Freedom means having a world of opportunity available to us — and the wisdom to be responsible in how we take advantage of those opportunities.
> Journalist, mother, proud American
>
> — **ESTHER CEPEDA**, Journalist

> Freedom means living in America pursuing my happiness via the God given individual rights guaranteed by the US Constitution as soon as we send the Obama gang packin'. 13
>
> — **TED NUGENT**, Musician

> Freedom —
> The stirring words of the Declaration of Independence are to me the best expression of freedom: "We hold these truths to be self evident, that all men are created equal".
> Julie Nixon Eisenhower
> daughter of the 37th President of the U.S.A.
>
> — **JULIE NIXON EISENHOWER**, Writer

> Freedom is the Bill of Rights, especially the First Amendment!
>
> — **LARRY KING**, Journalist d.2021

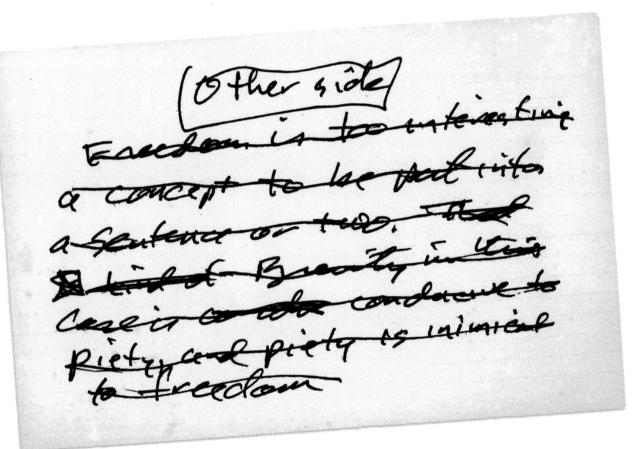

Back

> Freedom is too intestine a concept to be put into a sentence or two. Brevity on this subject is conducive to piety, and piety is inimical to freedom.
>
> — Norman Mailer

NORMAN MAILER
Writer, d.2007

Ted Cruz Rally, Atlanta

February 27, 2016

Through my 15 years of collecting Freedom Cards, I have gone to many political rallies. I carry around a clipboard for people to write cards on. This rally for Ted Cruz was held before Georgia voted on Super Tuesday in the Republican presidential primary.

THE FREEDOM CARDS

Freedom means the right to practice my faith in God without persecution.
Freedom means living our lives with the protection of the Constitution of the United States of America.
To live in a country of the Republic - life, liberty - choice.

ANONYMOUS

Do anything I desire as long as it does not infringe on any other person's freedom.

Henry L. Ashmire
Sharpsburg, GA 30277

HENRY ASHMIRE

Freedom means love for all people.

C.J.

C.J.

LIMITED GOVERNMENT

ANONYMOUS

World War II Homefront Poster
National Archives

THE FREEDOM CARDS

Medal of Honor Recipients

> Only with freedom can a country be a great country
>
> Paul J. Wiedorfer CMH
> US Army WWII
> 80th Infantry Division
> Chaumont, Belgium
> December 25, 1944

PAUL J. WIEDORFER
Medal of Honor, WWII, d.2011

> Ed Freeman
> "Freedom is number 1"

ED FREEMAN
Medal of Honor, Vietnam War d.2008

> Freedom is A OBLiGaTion THaT Todays Generation owes Tomorrows Generation. iT is PaRT of "THe PROmiSe" made To us By our fore-faThers.
>
> Sammy L Davis
> Medal of Honor
> Viet Nam 1967-68

SAMMY L. DAVIS
Medal of Honor, Vietnam War

> "If THE SON, THEREFORE, SHALL MAKE YOU FREE... YOU SHALL BE FREE, INDEED GOSPEL OF JOHN 8:36
>
> Gary Beikirch
> 5th Special Forces
> Medal of Honor
> Vietnam
> 4/1/70

GARY BEIKIRCH
Medal of Honor, Vietnam War

> Walter D. Ehlers
> Freedom means love for God and Country. The American Flag of the United States means freedom to more people than any other symbol in our world.

WALTER EHLERS
Medal of Honor, WWII, d.2014

> Freedom:
> To me is The Right of every american to say and do as they please. Even burn our flag, which I feel is very wrong... But THAT IS Freedom.
>
> Michael J. Fitzmaurice
> Medal of Honor Recipient.

MICHAEL FITZMAURICE
Medal of Honor, Vietnam War

> FREEDOM. MY COURSE TO NAVIGATE.
>
> William Swenson
> MOH 2013

WILLIAM D. SWENSON
Medal of Honor, War in Afghanistan

THE FREEDOM CARDS

World War II Homefront Poster
National Archives

THE FREEDOM CARDS

> Within each person resides the potential to challenge destiny waiting only for that mysterious time when events and circumstances so combine— FREEDOM allows each of us to find that potential and thereby change the world.
>
> *Paul Bucha, MOH RVN 1968*

PAUL BUCHA
Medal of Honor, Vietnam War

> We must all try to preserve the Freedom that so many Americans have sacrificed to allow us to enjoy the Freedom we have today.
>
> *Hiroshi H Miyamura "CMH" Korea 1951 U.S. Army 3rd Div.*

HIROSHI MIYAMURA
Medal of Honor, Korean War

> To me Freedom is the opportunity for my Children to live a life in a Country that allows them the individual pursuit of Education Prosperity and Joy. Mainly Freedom give me and my family the privilege of worshiping God as Free Christians.
>
> *Nick Bacon*

NICK BACON
Medal of Honor, Vietnam War, d.2010

> It is great to live in a country that will always be free.
>
> *M/Sgt Nicholas Oresko CMH Battle of The Bulge WWII 1-23-45*

NICHOLAS ORESKO
Medal of Honor, WWII, d.2013

> To me freedom means living in the greatest country in the world and the ability to go and do anything you would like to do without fear.
>
> *Walter J Marm Col US Army (Ret) Vietnam Veteran and Medal of Honor recipient Battle of IA DRANG. 14-17 Nov 65*

WALTER MARN
Medal of Honor, Vietnam War

> I am honored to have served with those willing to give their lives so we all can remain free.
>
> *Drew Dix US Army Special Forces*

DREW DIX
Medal of Honor, Vietnam War

> Freedom! We have it because of Our Constitution—let it not be Changed.
>
> *John Finn*

JOHN FINN
Medal of Honor, WWII, d.2010

> I enjoy freedom because Americans before me were willing to sacrifice their lives to establish, protect and preserve it for me. I am privileged. It is now my responsibility to protect and preserve Freedom, as we know it today, for future generations.
>
> *James Taylor, CMH Major U.S. Army (Ret)*

JAMES TAYLOR
Medal of Honor, Vietnam War

THE FREEDOM CARDS

World War II Homefront Poster
National Archives

THE FREEDOM CARDS

> Freedom should be cherished by all Americans. We should never forget that it has been given to us by others — by others who suffered, bled and died on battlefields, in the air and on the seas around the world — by others who held their nation and their comrades above themselves — by others who continue to serve for us so that we may live in freedom.
>
> Charles P. Murray
> Medal of Honor
> 3rd Infantry Division
> World War II
>
> 7/4/2007

CHARLES MURRAY
Medal of Honor, WWII, d.2011

> Freedom is the privilege to speak, pray, and live one's life as he wishes but without encroaching on others. We have the responsibility to act in any way necessary to preserve this blessing passed down to us through great wisdom, courage, sacrifice, and honor.
>
> T. Hudner Jr.
> Medal of Honor

THOMAS HUDNER
Medal of Honor, Korean War, d.2017

> The Freedom Project 25 Jan 07
> "You have never lived until you have almost died — For those who fought for 'Freedom': Life has a 'Special Flavor' the protected will never know"
>
> Ola L. Mize
> Col. (Ret) USASF
> Co. M, M.O.H.

OLA MIZE
Medal of Honor, Vietnam War

> Freedom means the right to do what you want. You and your country must be secure to enjoy freedom.
>
> Melvin E. Biddle
> C.M.H.
> PFC Co "B" 517th P.I.R.

MELVIN BIDDLE
Medal of Honor, WWII, d.2010

> Freedom is the basic building block that provides equality for each of its recipients. Country of origin, race or ethnic background are not limitations for one to enjoy Freedom. Freedom is a very fragile element to be guarded closely and protected!
>
> Harold A. Fritz
> Medal of Honor

HAROLD FRITZ
Medal of Honor, Vietnam War

> Freedom means being able to live in a land where we can help one another and grow to our full potential. I have been privileged to serve America in peace and war to defend our freedom.
>
> Robert B. Nett
> Col. U.S. Army Rangers

ROBERT NETT
Medal of Honor, WWII, d.2008

> There are so many freedoms in this country (to travel, religion, speech, etc.) denied in other countries that one does not enhance or diminish the others —
>
> Francis Curry

FRANCIS CURRY
Medal of Honor, WWII, d.2019

> Freedom is the reward we earn when our nation is more important than ourselves.
>
> Jack Jacobs
> Col, USA
> Ret

JACK JACOBS
Medal of Honor, Vietnam War

World War II Homefront Poster
National Archives

THE FREEDOM CARDS

Freedom is that myself & Family grow up to make our own decisions

— David A. McNerney, MOH
1/Sgt "A" 1/8 INF. 4TH INF. DIV.
VIETNAM 1967

DAVID MCNERNEY
Medal of Honor, Vietnam War

To Me Freedom is the ability To Choose how To Live, Worship, Vote and to Be all I can be By The Grace of God

— Allen J. Lynch MOH
D Co 1 BN 12 Cav 1st Cav Div
VIETNAM 6-67 TO 6-68
John 3:16-18

ALLEN LYNCH
Medal of Honor, Vietnam War

Freedom means waking safe with a chance to live your own dreams, speak your own mind and follow your own conscience. Freedom means not being afraid of losing life in the defense of those you love.

— Bob Kerrey

BOB KERREY
Medal of Honor, Vietnam War, Senator from Nebraska 1989-2001

Freedom is not free!

— Everett P. Pope
Medal of Honor
USMC
WWII

EVERETT POPE
Medal of Honor, WWII, d.2009

*Duane E. Dewey
M.O.H.   U.S.M.C.R.
KOREA   4-16-52
To me, freedom is everything with out it, We have nothing.*

DUANE E. DEWEY
Medal of Honor, Korean War

Our Freedom was fought for, Died for by our fore fathers who wrote our Constitution To protect us and our freedoms. To day our freedoms are being Threatened from many directions. Our Rights as laid out in the Constitution, are being overturned by Radicals, and other Leftist. Religion, the 2nd Amend, great Right To bear arms, and many others. I have faith that you and your Generation will overcome and Protect our Constitution bravely.

— Robert R. Ingram MOH

ROBERT INGRAM
Medal of Honor, Vietnam War

The greatest thing we gain from "Freedom" is the right to choose.

— Robert Lewis Howard
MEDAL of HONOR
VIETNAM, DECEMBER 1968

ROBERT HOWARD
Medal of Honor, Vietnam War, d.2009

Freedom is the building block of a democratic society. Worshiping God, Loving Country and Pursuing Happiness are all possible if liberty prevails. Without it, the pursuit becomes a journey that is directed by the whims of a dictator. Defend freedom with all your might and America will continue in greatness.

— Charles Coolidge
Belmont Sur Buttant, France
24-27 October 1944

CHARLES COOLIDGE
Medal of Honor, WWII, d.2021

> Freedom is not only realizing your potential, but it is also having the ability to reach that potential. I am the daughter of two Cuban immigrants working on my doctorate with the Freedom to think how I choose.

VICTORIA MENENDEZ
Dental Student

THE FREEDOM CARDS

Central Park, New York, New York

The Freedom Road Trip
Summer 2017

THE FREEDOM CARDS

STANSFIELD TURNER
Admiral in the Navy and CIA Director 1977-1981, d.2018

Freedom means the right to express your views openly —
Stan Turner
Adm, USN (Ret)
Ex Director of CIA

DON MALARKEY
Band of Brothers, WWII Veteran, d.2017

Freedom to me means the right to live in peace and responsibly —

FREDERICK BLESSE
General in the US Air Force, d.2012

— Freedom —
1. Freedom to me is to have the option to choose one's direction in life and then pursue it to the utmost of your ability.
2. Cherish your failures. If you are smart, you will learn the most from them.
Frederick C Blesse
M/Gen USAF (Ret)

STEPHEN BONNER
WWII Fighter Ace

To have the right to voice my opinion by ballot and to know I am heard.
Stephen Bonner
USAF ACE

JOHN WALKER
Vietnam Veteran

Freedom is the Ability to Live Your own Life As you wish And Allowing others To do so Too
Jon Walker
Forward observer 6" mm Arty
Co B 2/7 1st Air Cav Div.
22 X-Ray/22 Oh Bang
Nov 1965 RVN

RUSSELL GACKENBACH
WWII Air Force Navigator, d.2019

Freedom is being able to do what I want to do and when I want to do it without asking any person for permission.
Russell E Gackenbach
WWII Navigator

DEAN LADD
WWII Marine Veteran

Freedom is not free but must be appreciated and defended by each generation.
Dean Ladd
at age 96, I am likely the oldest retired Marine in the nation.

EUGENE DERRICOTTE
Tuskegee Airman

FREEDOM THAT PROVIDES US OPPORTUNITY TO ENJOY LIVING A LOVING AND CARING LIFE.
Gene Derricotte - Tuskegee Airman

44

Dear Alex,

I once heard a Dutch man in Eindhoven Holland define the word "Freedom" as he heard U.S., & G.I.'s talking about it. He said "You don't know what the word 'Freedom' means until you lose it." Having been under Nazi rule for 5 years he expressed it better than anyone I know

Fondest Regards
Edward Babe Heffron
Easy Co 506 Parachute Inf. Rgt
101st A.B.

ED HEFFRON
WWII Veteran, Band of Brothers, d.2013

THE FREEDOM CARDS

Edgar Mitchell on the Moon
The National Archives

THE FREEDOM CARDS

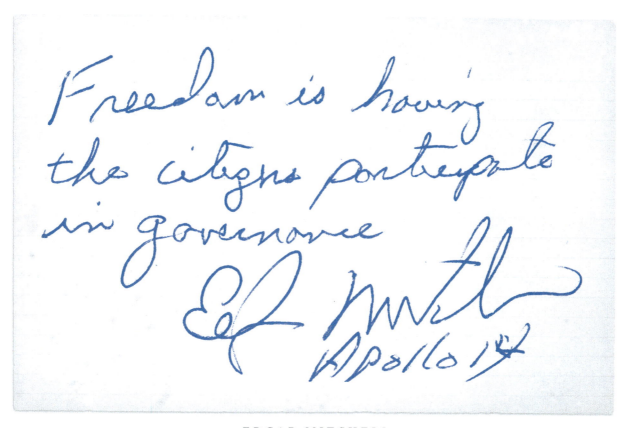

EDGAR MITCHELL
Astronaut and Moonwalker on Apollo 14

THE FREEDOM CARDS

I met Gale at a Bernie Sanders rally in
Columbia, South Carolina, on February 28, 2020.
"Equality and opportunity for all Americans to thrive."

THE FREEDOM CARDS

> Freedom is the right to fully live your human potential
>
> Michael V Hayden
> General, USAF (ret)
> D CIA

MICHAEL HAYDEN
CIA Director 2006-2009, NSA Director 1999-2005

> I DON'T REALLY KNOW WHAT FREEDOM REALLY IS... I'VE ONLY EVER LIVED IN AMERICA.
>
> Leslie James Pickering

LESLIE JAMES PICKERING
Activist, Spokesman for the Earth Liberation Front 1997-2002

> To me, "FREEDOM" is the privilege to enjoy life peacefully, healthfully and religiously in a beautiful country, with fellow Americans.
>
> Edith R. Yuellig

EDITH YUELLIG
My Grandma, d.2011

> Freedom is my right to believe in what and who I want to!
>
> [signature]

ANNALEIGH ASHFORD
Actor

> Freedom lets me be me and you be you
>
> Thomas DiNapoli

THOMAS DINAPOLI
Comptroller of New York

> I LOST MY FREEDOM FOR 1½ YEARS Being A Prisoner of War.
> I SAW MEN being STARVED AND being Worked To Death
> I WAS ON WHAT IS KNOWN AS "The Heydekrug RUN"
> Also I WAS ON "The German Death March" For 86 DAYS. Freedom is Not Free
> 8-4-2014
> Lester F. Schrenk

LESTER SCHRENK
WWII Veteran, POW

> FREEDOM MEANS I CAN TAKE CHARGE & DO WHAT'S RIGHT!

NORMAN SCHWARZKOPF
Army General and Gulf War Commander, d.2012

> Freedom is showing up and living in and with the nuances of our whole selves, unapologetically.
>
> Jeffreen M Hayes
> Curator & Arts Activist

JEFFREEN HAYES
Executive Director, Threewalls

THE FREEDOM CARDS

JENNIFER OSBON

Freedom to me means being able to express yourself and what you believe. It is truly a blessing

Rosemary Osbon
-14 years old

ROSEMARY OSBON

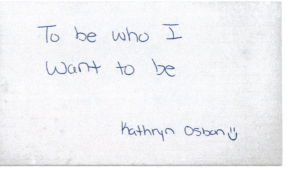

KATHRYN OSBON

Marco Rubio Rally,
Cobb County, Georgia

February 27, 2016

THE FREEDOM CARDS

Freedom means speaking my mind and hearing others do the same.
Bob Edwards
broadcast journalist

BOB EDWARDS
Journalist

Freedom to me means to live a life of liberty with all human rights accorded to everyone; Freedom from government coercion — the freedom to be whatever I choose. Helen Thomas

HELEN THOMAS
Journalist, d.2012

Freedom of Speech is Essential for true Democracy.
VICE

SHANE SMITH
Journalist, Founder Vice News

Freedom lets us each find our own way.
Dana Priest
4/2013

DANA PRIEST
Journalist

THE FREEDOM CARDS

Princeton University, Princeton, New Jersey

> A land of freedom is a land where chance alone does not determine one's lot in life. Even in the worst of times, America always has the potential to be the land of the free.
> And we should all help it get there. — Ethan Gordon (Miramar)
>
> — A Princeton Student, one of the luckiest people on Earth

ETHAN GORDON
Student

> Music, when done with heart, when shared with the right group of people, gives me freedom. So I'd have to say that freedom is whatever circumstances give me the ability to feel that spark of enlightenment and joy — it's a freedom that resonates with others and radiates beyond just myself.
>
> An extremely fortunate individual who plays with friends in the Princeton University Band

GLENDA CHEN
Student

The Freedom Road Trip
Summer 2017

FREEDOM IS
NO ONE HIT ME!
GOT IN MY WAY TO
I JUMPED OFF
BUILT MY WINGS
DOWN!
FREEDOM!

LOS ANGELES!
HANDCUFFED ME
BECOME ME!
A CLIFF AND
ON THE WAY

Ray Bradbury

RAY BRADBURY
Writer, d.2012

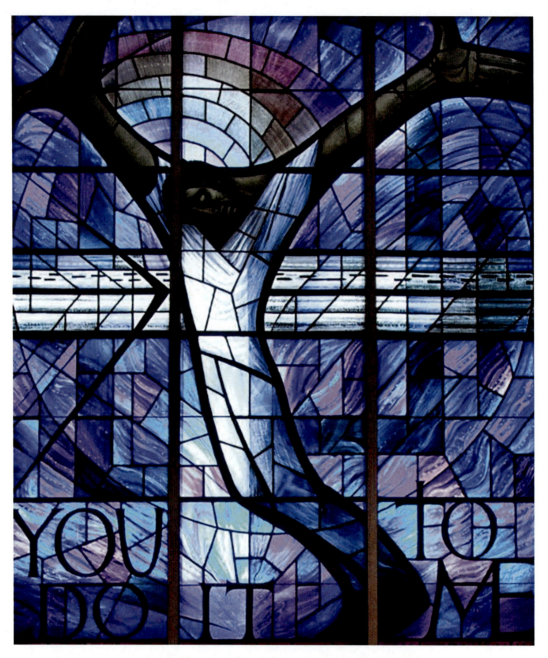

Stained Glass in the 16th Street Baptist Church
Photograph by Carol M. Highsmith, 16th Street Baptist Church, Birmingham, Alabama. 2010. Library of Congress Item 2010636939

> Sarah Collins Rudolph
> Freedom mean to live, love, and never be ashame of being different.

SARAH JEAN COLLINS
Survivor of the 16th Street Baptist Church Bombing, 1968

THE FREEDOM CARDS

> Freedom! Having the opportunity of opening a door from the inside, going out, and walking as far or for as long as you want.
> Ernie Brace
> POW Laos/VN 1965-1973

ERNIE BRACE
Vietnam Veteran and POW, d.2014

> We are all in this together — So every American should + will help for our collective efforts will prevail !!
> God Bless America
> July 2006
> Davy Jones

DAVY JONES
WWII Veteran, Doolittle Raider, POW, d.2008

> After enduring 7 months as a German POW in WWII, I have a greater sense of the true value and meaning of FREEDOM. I'm thankful to God and the USA for the

Front

> boundless opportunities I have had to choose the life I have lived.
> Sgt. Bob Bearden
> H.Co. 507 PIR 82nd Abn.
> Age 93

BOB BEARDEN — Back
WWII Veteran and POW, d.2017

THE FREEDOM CARDS

> As a former Vietnam POW of five and a half years, I know what it's like to lose your freedom. Without a doubt, freedom is our most precious heritage. We must be very diligent to protect it for those who follow us. God Bless America—
> Leon (Lee) Ellis, Col. USAF(Ret)

LEE ELLIS
Vietnam Veteran and POW

> What Freedom means to me. I was a P.O.W. of the N. Vietnam Aug 1967 – March 1973.
> Freedom is opening your door from the *inside* of the room!
> It is also that time when someone is not trying to kill you!
> Col. Bud Day MOH-AFC
> Author – Duty Honor Country

BUD DAY
WWII, Korean War, Vietnam Veteran, POW, d.2013

> As an Ex-POW, freedom was the ultimate joy and most wonderful moment of my life! Without freedom we do not really live.
> Ben Steele

BEN STEELE
WWII Veteran, POW, d.2018

> To live & love no matter what religion, race, sex or sexual orientation you are!!
> xx
> Former POW Iraqi Freedom

SHOSHANA JOHNSON
Iraq War Veteran, POW

59

One of the card files I carry with me when collecting cards.

THE FREEDOM CARDS

Two protestors at Donald Trump's Inauguration.

In the chaos of the protest, I wasn't able to get these two demonstrators' names.

THE FREEDOM CARDS

Freedom is everything!
James W. Baker III

JAMES BAKER III
Secretary of State 1989-1992

Freedom means the freedom to speak to worship, to VOTE! & The freedom to take politics SERIOUSLY! CA

CHRISTIANE AMANPOUR
Journalist

Freedom is the power and the right to act and think the way you want to without fear of restraint.
As a police officer I help protect a persons freedom to express themselves in a lawful manner.
Captain Joseph Shannon
Capt J. Shannon

JOSEPH SHANNON
Captain of Edison, NJ, Police Department

Freedom Means Eternal Vigilance
James O'Keefe
Undercover journalist
Muckraker. President of Project Veritas

JAMES O'KEEFE
Undercover Journalist, Activist

THE FREEDOM CARDS

> "Freedom" is the name of my guardian angel.
>
> *William Peter Blatty*

WILLIAM PETER BLATTY
Writer, *The Exorcist*

> Freedom means:
>
> Equal rights and protection from arbitrary government action under law. No exceptions.
>
> *W.M. Blumenthal*
> W. Michael Blumenthal
> Former U.S. Secretary of the Treasury

MICHAEL BLUMENTHAL
Secretary of the Treasury 1977-1979

> Freedom is liberation of the Human Spirit from inner-imposed limits and externally constrained ones by unjust authorities.

PHILIP ZIMBARDO
Psychologist, The Stanford Prison Experiment

> Freedom is the right to think, to believe, to speak, to hope and to chose who rules us. It also means respect for other peoples rights
>
> *George Robertson*
> Former Secretary General of NATO and UK Defence Secretary

GEORGE ROBERTSON
UK Defense Secretary 1997-1999, NATO Secretary General 1999-2004

> 7-11-17
> Freedom is the ability to do what you want, when you want, because you can!
>
> *Maureen Fullaway*
> Affordable Housing Manager
> Princeton, NJ

MAUREEN FULLAWAY
Affordable Housing Manager, Princeton, NJ

> Freedom is being able to live your truth without fear and with dignity.
>
> Colonel *Margarethe Cammermeyer* RN, PhD USA retired

MARGARETHE CAMMERMEYER
Washington National Guard, Activist

> Freedom to me is the opportunity and the rights to be whatever my god-given talents allows me to be here in the United States.
>
> *Steve Spurrier*
> S.C. Football Coach

STEVE SPURRIER
Former College Football Coach

> My freedom means to me: That I long for freedom for every human being and animal on earth.
>
> *Louise Fletcher*

LOUISE FLETCHER
Actress, *One Flew Over the Cuckoo's Nest*

Grant Park, Chicago, Illinois, Summer of 2017.
I was walking around Buckingham Fountain in Grant Park when I met Justin and Malcolm.
I don't know what they are up to today, but if you know them, send me a text.

THE FREEDOM CARDS

The american dream

MALCOLM EVANS

MALCOLM EVANS

A world where I still feel like I can save the world

Justin Finley

JUSTIN FINLEY

The Freedom Road Trip
Summer 2017

Notes from The Freedom Road Trip

It took two days to get to Morgantown. I had just tobogganed down the rust belt from Buffalo to Pittsburgh and finally made it to West Virginia. I stayed on back roads and stopped at every biker bar, library, and flower stand I passed. I'm sitting in a bar at my hotel writing this, watching endless Russian stories zip along the CNN ticker. A guy three seats down asked the bartender again about Trump.

"This land was made for you and me."
—Woody Guthrie

The summer felt like it had only just begun, but I had already made it past Upstate New York. As I passed by the white steeple churches of Stockton, New York, the roads were lined with pastel blue and yellow buildings, and the small in-town cemetery had just two narrow tire trenches that formed a dirt road. As I drove, I stopped at a gun club that seemed interesting from the road. After parking, I could see the members staring. I walked up to the club's porch, and one of the members asked me after a brief introduction, "Are you a liberal?"

I squirmed away as I concealed my answer with a smile. No one joined our conversation. The members seemed nice enough—although one lady followed me around like she was a security guard. I think she was googling The Freedom Cards on her phone, because her eyes jumped back and forth between my bag and her cell phone screen.

A couple of the guys took me around their headquarters, which was a large trailer nicely painted. The first room was a large meeting space with foldable white tables, while the second was filled from floor to ceiling with foam and plastic animals used for target practice. There were hundreds, including deer, turkeys, boars, and others less typical like a large king cobra.

"I beg you, discover this country."
—Maya Angelou

I asked to see the shooting range, and one gentleman led me out through a soft wet path towards the woods. We talked about gun control, and he seemed open to my project and what we were hoping to accomplish. He was weatherworn and had a camouflage hat pulled down, concealing most of his eyes. He stopped me at the first shooting range, which looked like a tunnel in the woods that ended with a deer target. Here, the sportsmen would play a golf-like game where they would shoot their bows and get points based on their accuracy. The lady guard continued to follow us deep into the forest. For a moment, I felt afraid alone in the woods, well-worn paths crossing well-worn paths.

THE FREEDOM CARDS

I returned to the trailer to make my pitch about the cards and collect as many as possible. The American flag waved from the railing. I handed out my clipboards, and the men started to write. As they wrote, they shared a disparaging comment about gun control and decried plans by Barack Obama and Andrew Cuomo. I took a picture of one of the men in front of the American flag holding his card.

> *"America! I do not vaunt my love for you. I have what I have."*
> —Walt Whitman

A new guy sat down a couple of seats from me at the hotel. He was selling financial products. I felt like I had heard the same conversation in Boston. My phone buzzed, and I hoped that it was a girl I had given my number to in New Haven, but it was just a CNN notification with more Trump news.

> *"America never was America to me."*
> —Langston Hughes

BERNARD DAKYMGELE
Bear Lake Rod and Gun Club Member

The Freedom Road Trip
Summer 2017

THE FREEDOM CARDS

> Freedom is being able to be who you are without fear of being mocked for your race, religion or sexuality

ELTON JOHN
Musician

THE FREEDOM CARDS

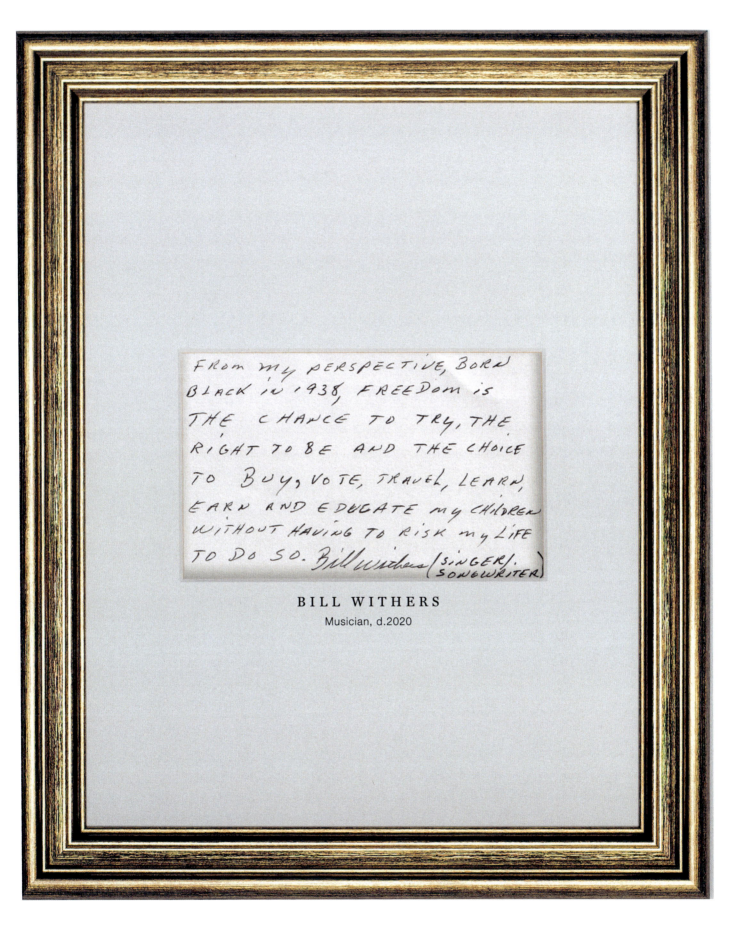

BILL WITHERS
Musician, d.2020

THE FREEDOM CARDS

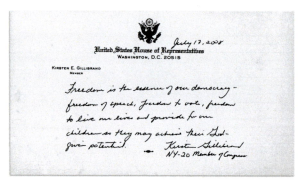

SHELLEY MOORE CAPITO
Senator

KIRSTEN GILLIBRAND
Senator

Both Shelley Moore Capito and Kirsten Gillibrand completed cards when they served as Representatives and are now Senators.

THE FREEDOM CARDS

TOMMY LEE
Musician

"You can't possibly appreciate freedom until it's been taken away..."
— Tommy Lee, Mötley Crüe

SANDRA FLUKE
Lawyer and Activist

"Freedom is an essential, but insufficient ingredient in full equality. We must work to ensure our citizens also have the means to effectuate their dreams and do not face inequitable barriers."
— Sandra K. Fluke, Social Justice Attorney

RHONDA FLEMING
Actress

"To me — freedom is the right to acknowledge that only with God's direction can we preserve and protect our precious freedom as our forefathers proclaimed it for America."
— Rhonda Fleming, Actress/Philanthropist

MALCOLM GLADWELL
Writer

"Freedom to me means the time and space to dream."
— Malcolm Gladwell, Author
Dec 1/16

JEFF STAHLER
Editorial Cartoonist

"The freedom of not eavesdropping on others..."
— Jeff Stahler, The Columbus Dispatch, United Feature Syndicate

SHELDON HARNICK
Songwriter

"In America, thank Heaven, we are free to express our opinions, politically and every other way. And although we may invite problems from those who disagree with us, at least our Government may not interfere with the expression of those opinions!"
— Sheldon Harnick

PHYLLIS COATES
Actress

"Freedom to me means: no Radicals in my country — We people obeying our laws & loving the USA."
— Phyllis Coates

JAKE GARN
Astronaut and Senator

"Freedom gave me the opportunity to be a United States Senator and an astronaut on the Space Shuttle Discovery."
— Jake Garn

THE FREEDOM CARDS

> Freedom affords the human spirit a chance to explore the reaches of its full potential. It liberates the life of the mind. It is an essential human right.
> —Carol Moseley Braun
> 27 May 2013

CAROL MOSELEY BRAUN
Senator from Illinois 1993-1999

> Everything!
> —Max Cleland
> 2013

MAX CLELAND
Senator from Georgia 1997-2003

> Freedom means "Magnificent America." I arrived in the U.S. at 5 in 1935 from Germany. Of my family that stayed behind, one survived WWII. So "Magnificent America" means life & freedom. To the world "Magnificent American" means peace. The 68 years since WWII is the longest period of peace without a war between major powers in history.
> —Rudy Boschwitz, U.S. Senator 1978-91
> Ambassador to the UN Human Rights Commission 2005

RUDY BOSCHWITZ
Senator from Minnesota 1978-1991

> Freedom means is is safe to be unpopular
> —Adlai Stevenson

ADLAI STEVENSON III
Senator from Illinois 1970-1981

> "Freedom is the essence of America, the opportunity for every American to live the American Dream."
> —Edward M. Kennedy
> United States Senator - Massachusetts

EDWARD KENNEDY
Senator from Massachusetts 1962-2009, d.2009

> With freedom you have hope. With hope, your dreams become possible.
> —Tom Harkin

TOM HARKIN
Senator from Iowa 1985-2015

> THOSE WHO BELITTLE FREEDOM ARE THOSE DESTINED TO LOSE IT!
> —Ben Nighthorse Campbell
> Retired U.S. Senator
> Captain US Olympic Judo Team
> Northern Cheyenne Chief Society

BEN NIGHTHORSE CAMPBELL
Senator from Colorado 1993-2005

> Freedom is the very essence of our quality of life. The more one is free, the more one is empowered.
> —Tom Daschle

TOM DASCHLE
Senator from South Dakota 1987-2005

THE FREEDOM CARDS

> Freedom to me is being able to live my life with Joy! To live my life with Peace! To live my life with all of God's Children with love and respect for our differences and rejoice!
> Sincerely,
> Mayor Beverly White

BEVERLY WHITE
Mayor of Lewisburg, WV

> FREEDOM MEANS TAKING TIME TO PRAISE, HONOR AND THANK OUR MILITARY PERSONNEL AND VETERANS FOR OUR WAY OF LIFE.
> FREEDOM MEANS AMERICA, GOD BLESS THE UNITED STATES OF AMERICA!
> Mayor Ken Miyagishima
> MAYOR KEN MIYAGISHIMA 11-08-2020

KEN MIYAGISHIMA
Mayor of Las Cruces, NM

> Freedom is essential for Life, Liberty and the Pursuit of Happiness.
> Jack Blalock
> Mayor of Portsmouth, N.H.

JACK BLAOCK
Mayor of Portsmouth, NH

> Freedom is being free from FEAR, enabling the pursuit of life, liberty & happiness!
> John Tecklenburg

JOHN TECKLENBURG
Mayor of Charleston, SC

> To me, freedom means having the ability to be who you are, to learn and grow and realize your full potential, without restriction or interference.
> Mike Purzycki
> Mayor, Wilmington, Del.

MIKE PURZYCKI
Mayor of Wilmington, DE

> Freedom means the ability to make my own choices and to accept sole responsibility for them.
> Michael E. Passero
> Mayor of New London

MICHAEL PASSERO
Mayor of New London, CT

> Freedom allows me the privilege and opportunity to make a meaningful, lasting impact on the lives of others.
> Allan Fung
> Mayor, Cranston, RI

ALLAN FUNG
Mayor of Cranston, RI

> Freedom means the opportunity to compete using your god-given talents.
> Mayor of the City of Richmond, VA

LEVAR STONEY
Mayor of Richmond, VA

Robson fights for freedom

By: Jonathan Mayran

ROBSON FLIPS through his large collection of Freedom Cards. He has received cards from many famous people today.

Regis Philbin

Alex Trebek

Senior Alex Robson wanted to know what freedom means to famous people in America. Through his freedom card project he has answered that question by writing to celebrities and politicians. He has received responses from people ranging from famous politicians, such as Zell Miller, to famous TV hosts, such as Regis Philbin from the shows "Who Wants to Be A Millionaire" and "Live With Regis and Kelly." The hardest response for him to receive was Jon Stewart's because Stewart doesn't normally sign autographs. All these people's freedom cards can be found at Robson's website DefineFreedom.com.

"I first started the Freedom Cards project when I first wrote a letter to Ken Starr and asked him to write what freedom meant to him. It intrigued me, so I continued to ask more and more people," Robson said.

At this point, he has spent around $750 of his own money toward his project. The cost includes $1 envelopes, stamps, and web hosting. From writing people, Robson has been able to meet Bill Elliot, the White House once called him, and Newt Gingride sent him an e-mail. Robson has been working on this project for almost five months. He is loving every minute of it, and one day hopes to display some of his work in the school.

continued on pg. 4

Dr. Wylie: essential as gravity

By: Radhika Solanki

Dr. Clyde Wylie's day starts out by teaching college prep and honors physics to juniors and ends by working with the Key Club. He values and cherishes his wife and kids and never gets tired of going to work. This year, Wylie was named Teacher of the Year at Mill Creek.

He considers teaching his purpose in life. "As I got into teaching, it was probably a year or so into teaching that I realized that I could do something and be a good teacher." Students also believe he is a fair educator. "He's a good teacher. He's one of those teachers that gives you equal credit. If you do the work, he's always there to help you," junior Brittany Brooks said.

Wylie was born in Kilbourne, a small town in Louisiana. Growing up, he lived with his mother, grandmother and four sisters. Wylie was an intelligent student, and was involved in many sports and clubs. He wanted to be involved in a lot of activities because of opportunities to see other parts of the world. Wylie attended a junior college in southern Mississippi and went to the University of Arkansas. He also went to Northeast Louisiana University. In college he

continued on pg. 3

Article published about The Freedom Cards in my high school newspaper.

On The Freedom Road Trip, I stayed at people's homes that I found on Airbnb. I sometimes stayed in the least expensive place I could find. For one night, I slept in the loft of this shed in Maskell, Nebraska. Maskell is a village that has a gun shop, a Lutheran church, and the smallest city hall in the United States.

NATIONAL REVIEW, 215 LEXINGTON AVENUE, NEW YORK, N.Y. 10016
Wm. F. Buckley Jr., Editor-at-Large   (212) 679-7330

Freedom makes life possible.

WFBuckley

WILLIAM F. BUCKLEY
Conservative Intellectual, d.2008

> Freedom means living in a country ruled by the great United States Constitution. It is the inspired recipe for liberty.
>
> Phyllis Schlafly

PHYLLIS SCHLAFLY
Conservative Activist, d.2016

Real freedom is liberty and accepting, respect and defend Personal freedom from or preserved the responsibilities a free country

"Having personal the obligation to the liberty of others cannot be separated without fulfilling of citizenship."

Robert M Gates
Secretary of Defense
2006 - 2011

ROBERT GATES
Secretary of Defense 2006-2011

The Coast of Oregon

If there is a God, he is undoubtedly there, where the ocean meets the mountains on dark sand beaches. Gusts of salty air push against the tall evergreen trees that latch onto the cliffs with roots 500 years old.

And cyclists ride up and down the hills with bikes packed like mules. And road turnoffs are filled with Toyota Tacomas and Subaru hatchbacks with people looking out far in the distance where the sea turns into the sky.

I am sitting and looking at the jagged outcroppings of stones where there is no Donald Trump or Barack Obama. No cancer or depression or bills past due.

It is just you and your skin and your eyes.

From my journal I took during The Freedom Road Trip

THE FREEDOM CARDS

81

**The Freedom
Road Trip**
Summer 2017

The night of May 29, 2020, was chaotic and loud. It began the nationwide Black Lives Matter protests that lasted months. I spoke with this man, and people began graffitiing the CNN letters and throwing rocks. I didn't get his name or his card, but he told me, *"In America, a black man is not free."*

THE FREEDOM CARDS

Freedom is how we respect the dignity of every human soul.
— Deval Patrick, Governor of Massachusetts

DEVAL PATRICK
Governor of Massachusetts 2007-2015

Freedom is having the right to have your own thought. To Dream and run for that dream
3/7/07

HERSCHEL WALKER
Football Player

"Freedom is the right to lead your life as you wish within the confines of the law".

Harry F. Byrd Jr. (Virginia)
(Former U.S. Senator
1965 – 1983)

HARRY BYRD JR.
US Senator from Virginia 1965-1983

Freedom is unity of Africans an a free Africa.
— Willie Ricks "Mukasa"

WILLIE RICKS
Civil Rights Activist

Freedom, to me means, the right to speak and express myself any time and any place.
— Laffit Pincay Jr., Jockey

LAFFIT PINCAY JR.
Jockey

As the grandson of a sharecropper, freedom provided the opportunity to pursue education & opportunities to reach for the stars!
— Mike Fossum, NASA Astronaut
STS-121, 124 ISS Exp 28/29

MICHAEL FOSSUM
Astronaut

Freedom represents and embodies the realization of human dignity in community.
— Ken Starr

KEN STARR
Solicitor General 1989-1993, Special Counsel 1994-1998

Freedom allows me to express a point of view that might not be politically correct, but will not threaten my livelihood as a Writer
— Gay Talese

GAY TALESE
Writer

84

THE FREEDOM CARDS

On April 23, 2016, a group gathered to hold a "pro-white" rally. Many came to counter-protest. I ran with them through the woods to confront the group.

Being able to do as you please.

ANONYMOUS
Stone Mountain, GA

> True freedom permits you to express your own personal opinions on any subject without fear of those who have the right to disagree.
>
> Freedom permits you to choose your own religion, politics as long as long as they are expressed with courtesy and respect for the rights of others.
>
> —John Wooden, UCLA

JOHN WOODEN
UCLA Basketball Coach 1948-1975, d.2010

THE FREEDOM CARDS

Freedom is being able to think & dream big & to take action to achieve your dream. — Dabo Swinney

DABO SWINNEY
Clemson Football Coach

FREEDOM PROVIDES US ALL THE CHANCE TO MAKE OUR OWN CHOICES FOR OUR OWN LIVES.
CHARLIE STRONG

CHARLIE STRONG
College Football Coach

Greatness - being able to [illegible]
U.S.A. — AND MAKE CHOICES

MIKE DITKA
NFL Player and Coach

Freedom means having the ability to express who you are (however you see fit) and who do you want to become in life (if the two are different). — Mike Brown

MIKE BROWN
NBA Associate Head Coach, Golden State Warriors

FREEDOM TO ME MAKES EACH BREATH TASTE GOOD. WE ALL NEED TO THANK THOSE WHO HELPED ACHIEVE IT.
— TERRY COLLINS
NY METS

TERRY COLLINS
MLB Manager and Coach

I chose baseball as my career. No one told me to or said I had to. That is the tip of the iceberg of what freedom is. Freedom of choice!?!
Don Zimmer
59 years in professional baseball.

DON ZIMMER
Major League Baseball 1854-2014, d.2014

Freedom means the opportunity to utilize our God-given talents to honor Him in a way that helps other people. — Tony Dungy

TONY DUNGY
NFL Coach

Freedom means to me the right to live life with the ability to "Love" all.

RON RIVERA
NFL Coach, Washington Football Team

THE FREEDOM CARDS

The National Archives

88

THE FREEDOM CARDS

> For me it's the freedom and respect us women enjoy in this Country with every opportunity to advance in any field of our choice.

ELINOR OTTO
Last Rosie the Riveter

THE FREEDOM CARDS

> The freedom afforded the individual in this country at least in regard to freedom of expression has allowed me to write about anything I want without having to worry about ~~official censorship~~, prison, or, ~~in some parts of the world~~, worse. I've taken full advantage of the freedom we have here in this and I'm very grateful for it. (over)

Front

> Feb 7, 2007
> Freedom under the Constitution means two very different things. The first — a very ancient liberty — is the freedom to take part in government. That's called democracy. The second — a more modern liberty — is the freedom

Front

> Something about myself.
> Randy Newman
> I'm a musician. I write songs, make records (or whatever you call them now), and write music for motion pictures. In a number of my songs, the narrator is unreliable, and sometimes is vulgar, pigheaded, bigoted, stupid & human.

RANDY NEWMAN
Musician
Back

> to lead our lives free of government control — for example freedom of speech. If our government is to work both kinds of freedom are necessary: an active participation in civic life and protection against tyranny — even (the tyranny of the majority)
> Stephen Breyer

STEPHEN BREYER
Supreme Court Justice
Back

90

THE FREEDOM CARDS

I wish so much that I could agree with your theme, "Every American has one thing in common... freedom."

Freedom means being part of nature, and pollution too often comes between us and even air and water.

Freedom means the power to choose, but young people now graduate with such huge debt — just to get the education given freely in

Front

other prosperous countries — that they must often enter into jobs they wouldn't otherwise choose.

Freedom means governance over one's own body, but the current U.S. government tries to prevent women of that — here and in other countries.

So I cherish relative freedom, and use it to gain true freedom, and a world in which everyone matters.

Gloria Steinem

GLORIA STEINEM
Women's Rights Activist

Back

FREEDOM MEANS YOU AND I ARE FREE TO LIVE AND LEAD OUR OWN LIVES. YOU MAY NOT STEAL FROM OTHERS AND THEY AS INDIVIDUALS OR THROUGH ANY GANG OR GOVERNMENT MAY NOT STEAL YOUR PROPERTY, YOUR INCOME, YOUR

Front

LIFE OR YOUR FUTURE.

EVERYONE KEEPS THEIR HANDS TO THEMSELVES. NO HITTING. HUGGING ALLOWED

FREEDOM IS LIFE. LIMITS ON FREEDOM ARE LIMITS ON LIFE.

GROVER NORQUIST
Activist

Back

> This country is not free like it used to be. There are new restrictions on what you can do with your land. —Jodie Jordan

JODIE JORDAN
Cape Elizabeth, Maine
(I wrote this card out for Mr. Jordan)

THE FREEDOM CARDS

Jody is a farmer and lobsterman in Cape Elizabeth, Maine.
He has a sign on his driveway that says,
"Keep driving. The chickens will move."

The Freedom Road Trip
Summer 2017

THE FREEDOM CARDS

> Freedom is being able to do what — after thinking clearly and calmly — we most want to do. But it can't be unlimited, because what I most want to do may prevent you doing what you most want to do. Peter Singer

PETER SINGER
Philosopher

> Freedom is living with no limitations, and being exactly who you want to be inside and out, without following no one, just being you!

MEL B
Musician, The Spice Girls

> To me, Freedom means you are responsible for your success, happiness and your future. You cannot remain free if you hold the Government or others responsible for your success, failure or happiness.
> Lou Holtz

LOU HOLTZ
Former Notre Dame Football Coach

> TRUE FREEDOM is the complicated negotiation between what I want and what we all want and need.
> Ken Burns

KEN BURNS
Documentary Film Maker

> Freedom is the ability to live our fullest human potential without interference and without interfering with the ability of others to reach theirs.
> Garry Kasparov
> May 2, 2016
> New York

GARRY KASPAROV
Russian Chess Grandmaster

> Freedom means to me to be "set free from enslavement to corruption and have the glorious freedom of the children of GOD" promised at Romans 8:21 and then having the freedom to live "forever" on a paradise "earth". PS. 37:29
> Margaret Keane March 2017
> My paintings and life were the subject of Tim Burton's movie "BIG EYES" in which Amy Adams won a Golden Globe award for Best Actress for her portrayal & role.
> Margaret Keane

MARGARET KEANE
Artist

> Freedom means liberation and the right to make choices, the right to be safe. Freedom means the right to dream and the chance to actualize those dreams.
> Candice Elder
> — Candice Elder, Activist
> East Oakland Collective

CANDICE ELDER
Activist, Founder, and CEO of The East Oakland Collective

> America is the Land of Freedom. Without Freedom I would of never became who I am Today!
> HOF 99   Orlando Cepeda

ORLANDO CEPEDA
Major League Baseball 1958-1974

THE FREEDOM CARDS

> FREEDOM IS EVERYTHING — THINK ABOUT IT.
> *Grace Slick*
> SARCASTIC BUT MOVING

GRACE SLICK
Musician

> Freedom from: oppression, from want, from discrimination, from undue surveillance. Freedom to: be — within moral & legal bounds — Live as I please, with whom I please & allowed to express myself freely.
> *Edward Albee*

EDWARD ALBEE
Playwright, d. 2016

> FREEDOM MEANS ACCEPTING AND EMBRACING ALL HUMAN BEINGS AS EQUALS WHO ARE MADE IN THE IMAGE OF GOD; AND WHO ALL HAVE A RIGHT TO QUALITY EDUCATION, HEALTH CARE AND A LIVING WAGE
>
> Dr. JEREMIAH A. WRIGHT
> PASTOR EMERITUS
> TRINITY UCC
> CHICAGO

JEREMIAH WRIGHT
Pastor

> "FREEDOM" IS THE ABSOLUTE RIGHT TO "BE ONE'S SELF" — A CONCEPT WHICH, TO ME, IS THE CORE AND ESSENCE OF A CIVILIZED SOCIETY!
> *Ronald G. Wayne*

RONALD WAYNE
Co-founder of Apple

> Freedom means being able to cross all boundaries, and touch someone's life. And inspire them to greatness
> *Otis Williams*
> Temptations 5/7/07

OTIS WILLIAMS
Musician, The Temptations

> Freedom is owning your life — the good & the bad.

PATTON OSWALT
Actor & Comedian

> To me, freedom is about endless possibilities and unlimited opportunities to live a fulfilling life.
> *Mario Andretti, 2007*
> Race car driver

MARIO ANDRETTI
Race Car Driver

> Freedom is rooted in the heart of every man. That freedom enables us to strive for excellence everyday without fear —
> *Bill Richardson*
> Governor of New Mexico

BILL RICHARDSON
Governor of New Mexico 2003-2011

435th Field Maintenance Squadron members set up a welcome-home sign for the homecoming of the 52 former hostages after their release from Iran in 1981.

National Archives photo no. 6344598

THE FREEDOM CARDS

> Freedom to me is evident in my right to speak my mind and be respected for doing so.
>
> Bruce Laingen
>
> I was the senior hostage in the Hostage Crisis in Tehran 1979-'81.

BRUCE LAINGEN
Hostage During the Iran Hostage Crisis

> Freedom means the ability to pursue a life of redeeming social value.
>
> THOMAS L. AHERN

THOMAS AHERN
Hostage During the Iran Hostage Crisis

To live life to the fullest no worries to come or for the rest of our days To live in peace and struggle when need

Joshua
Joshua Crosby

JOSHUA CROSBY
Blackville, SC

Evan interviewed me on the steps of the Lincoln Memorial.

Right to speak your mind, & respect differences

Reporter, WUSA9, D.C.

EVAN KOSLOF
Journalist, Washington, D.C.

THE FREEDOM CARDS

> freedom means being able to be yourself no matter who or what is around!
> alisha wiley!
>
> I am an awesome person

ALISHA WILEY
Princeton, NJ

Alisha worked at Blue Mountain Coffee. Blue Mountain hosted me for freedom events throughout the East Coast.

> Freedom means to me "what God Triune my Creator – Savior wants of me = i.e to love God Triune with all my heart and my neighbor as my self!

FATHER THOMAS SMITH
Monastery of the Holy Spirit, Conyers, GA

The Freedom Road Trip
Summer 2017

THE FREEDOM CARDS

What does freedom mean to an extremist?

The six cards on the opposite page are from people who appear on the Southern Poverty Law Center's Extremists List.

THE FREEDOM CARDS

```
Freedom is doing my duty.
I decide what is my duty.
I decide how to do this duty.

Gerhard Lauck
RJG Ennterprises Inc
```

GERHARD LAUCK
Neo-Nazi Activist

Freedom is precious, but at least as important is what we do with it. Better to do what is right with less freedom, than to do evil with more.

Mark Weber
Writer, publisher
July 28, 2020

MARK WEBER
Holocaust-Denying Historian

Freedom is the ability to learn from your mistakes and to be a better person than you were the day before

Morris Golett
Free man

MORRIS GOLETT
Aryan Nation Leader

Freedom is putting duty & honor above personal self interest.
Michael Hill, Chief,
League of the South

7-21-20

MICHAEL HILL
Chief of the League of the South

What Freedom means to me: The Individual's ability to use his/hers God-Given Free Will while protected by Government from the restrictions of Arbitrary Force.
Tom DeWeese, President, American Policy Center

TOM DEWEESE
Antigovernment Activist

Having the courage to swim against the tide is freedom to me.

James Edwards

JAMES EDWARDS
Right-Wing Podcaster

THE FREEDOM CARDS

JAN JOHNSON CARYLE
Rim of Grand Canyon, Arizona

Jan was visiting Las Vegas for a family reunion.

Jerry was stocking his farm stand when he completed his Freedom Card.

JERRY DUNAFIN
Stroh, Indiana

THE FREEDOM CARDS

Mireya was selling cowboy boots and hats to tourists when I met her.

IT MEANS TO DO ANYTHING YOU WANT WITH OUT WORRY ABOUT ANYTHING.

Mireya
A LATIN GIRL LIVING IN JACKSON WY.

MIREYA
Jackson Hole, Wyoming

Come and go as you please. Say what you want to. Do what you want without reason. Go state to state.
Mark Swift

MARK SWIFT
Kenosha, Wisconsin

I didn't see Mark catch any fish.

The Freedom Road Trip
Summer 2017

THE FREEDOM CARDS

> FREEDOM IS WHERE YOUR DREAMS TAKE YOU
> *[signature]*
> NASCAR

KYLE PETTY
NASCAR Driver & Race Team CEO

> Freedom means life, liberty and the pursuit of happiness for everyone.
> *Betty M. James*
> Slinky's Mother

BETTY JAMES
Inventor of the Slinky

> Where there is equal access and equal opportunity, freedom means an open door to develop talents through education and meaningful performance that maintains our countries strengths and values.
> *Charles E. McGee, Col USAF (Ret.)*
> Tuskegee Airman

CHARLES MCGEE
Tuskegee Airmen

> Freedom means suffering of coercion not consented to.
> *[signature]*

GEORGE WILL
Writer and Political Commentator

> FREEDOM IS TO CREATE!
> *[signature]*
> CHARLIE ADLARD IS THE ARTIST OF THE WALKING DEAD.

CHARLIE ADLARD
Comic Book Artist, *The Walking Dead*

> FREEDOM IS life, liberty & the pursuit of HAPPINESS...
> *[signature]*
> Former Nixon White House Counsel

JOHN DEAN III
White House Council 1970-1973

> FREEDOM ALLOWS US TO HAVE AN OPEN MIND AND KEEP IT!
> BIG BIRD OF SESAME STREET AND *Caroll Spinney* WHO KNOWS B.BIRD FROM THE INSIDE. — OCT. '06

CAROLL SPINNEY
Puppeteer and Actor, d.2018

> Freedom is voting without hindrance.
> *Sonia Manzano*
> Author/Actor

SONIA MANZANO
Author and Actor

THE FREEDOM CARDS

Freedom means being in control of your own destiny.

Pasquale Buzzelli

PASQUALE BUZZELLI
9/11 Survivor

Freedom is mental only. It doesn't matter if you're locked up, or a billionaire —

John D.
DRUMMER FOR "THE DOORS"

JOHN DENSMORE
Musician, The Doors

Freedom is Equality

(i.e., ensuring that those with the power are subjected to the same burdens they impose on the powerless.)

Minister and Equal Protection Activist

———— Mike Newdow

MIKE NEWDOW
Activist

Freedom is the Gift of God which when exercised allows us to create the tomorrows in which we live
John Ashcroft

JOHN ASHCROFT
Attorney General 2001-2005

Poker game in Fremont, MI.

THE FREEDOM CARDS

The Freedom Road Trip
Summer 2017

THE FREEDOM CARDS

CLINT HILL
US Secret Service

JAMES LEAVELLE
Police Officer, Dallas, TX

GENE BOONE
Sheriff, Dallas, TX

RONALD JONES
Doctor, Dallas, TX

THE FREEDOM CARDS

The National Archives

> Freedom is the ability to express ones self without fear of retribution

JAMES TAGUE
Injured During the JFK Assassination

> Freedom is the lifeblood of America ... the most valuable component that sets this nation apart from almost all others.
>
> Hugh Aynesworth
> (Reporter, Writer & Author)

HUGH AYNESWORTH
Dallas Journalist

> Freedom, to me, means being able to read and discover the God of my Bible.
>
> Mary Ann Moorman

MARY ANN MOORMAN
Witness to the JFK Assassination

> Freedom in a true democracy is a guarantee that you will not be persecuted or prosecuted because of your race, religion, ethnicity, or political beliefs. Freedom includes and assures the right to be physically safe from unfettered police misconduct and to have civil and criminal justice systems that function fairly and objectively.
> (20 Mar 07)   Cyril H. Wecht, M.D., J.D.

CYRIL WECHT
Forensic Pathologist

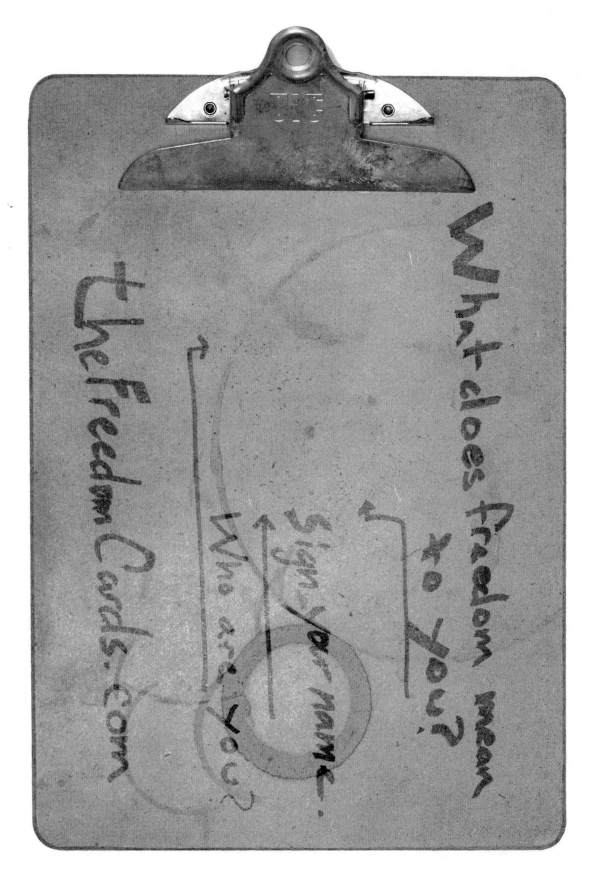

My first clipboard for traveling and collecting cards, approximately 2012-2015.

THE FREEDOM CARDS

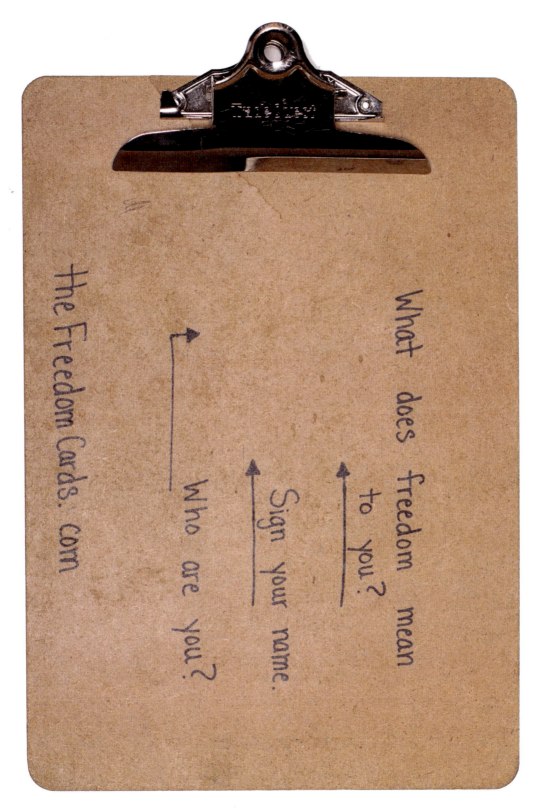

My ex-girlfriend wrote this one. She just got married a few weeks ago. I saw her recently at an Atlanta Hawks game, and when she noticed me, she quickly put her hand in her pocket to hide her engagement ring. I'm not sure why—maybe she thought it would upset me, or perhaps just common courtesy? In any case, I'm still using the clipboard.

THE FREEDOM CARDS

Republican National Convention, July 19, 2016, Cleveland, Ohio

> Having the opportunity to freely pursue our dreams.
>
> Laura Veira
> Student

LAURA VEIRA
Protestor

> FREEDOM TO ME IS LIVING FREELY WITH THE FOUNDATION OF THE CONSTITUTION AND THE DEMOCRATIC PROCESS THAT THIS COUNTY WAS BUILT ON.
>
> Jack Dunn

JACK DUNN
Bikers for Trump

> Freedom Means Leave Me Alone if I'm not bothering you.
> Micah Naziri

MICAH NAZIRI
Protestor

> is a state of being.
> Vermin Supreme

VERMIN SUPREME
Presidential Candidate

112

THE FREEDOM CARDS

Republican National Convention

July 19, 2016, Cleveland, Ohio

> Freedom means having a Strong National Defense so no one can attack us.
>
> Joan Smith

JOAN SMITH
RNC Attendee

> THE ABILITY TO DISAGREE WITH EACH OTHER & STILL SIT DOWN TO A GREAT MEAL TOGETHER
>
> CALVIN D. WILLIAMS
> CLEVELAND DIVISION OF POLICE JULY 2016

CALVIN WILLIAMS
Cleveland Chief of Police

> FREEDOM LIVING WITHOUT INTERFERANCE AND DOING THE SAME FOR OTHERS
>
> Tom Tuck

TOM TUCK
Montana Delegation

Republican National Convention, July 19, 2016, Cleveland, Ohio

THE FREEDOM CARDS

On March 24th, 2020, I ventured into the silent streets of the first COVID lockdown. Outside of one of the new testing locations, Karia completed a card. It reads: *"Freedom to me means having a piece [peace] from worries. Freedom to love, speak, and care for one another."*

THE FREEDOM CARDS

> FREEDOM IS BEING ABLE TO DRAW FUNNY PICTURES OF POWERFUL PEOPLE, WHO DON'T THINK THEY ARE FUNNY PICTURES, AND NOT HAVE TO WORRY ABOUT GOING TO JAIL OR BEING DEPORTED BACK TO CANADA
>
> POLITICAL CARTOONIST

PAUL SZEP
Political Cartoonist for the Boston Globe from 1967-2001

> We are so very blessed to know what Freedom is here in the United States! I think of all the diversity & individuals that Freedom allows us to be!
>
> #27 USA Softball

JENNIE FINCH
Team USA Softball 2004, 2008

> Freedom is the right to Equality for all — The right to decisions about your body, sexuality & birthright!

KATHY NAJIMY
Actress

> Freedom is freedom of speech, freedom of thought, and (as Franklin Roosevelt said) also freedom from want.

EDWARD WITTEN
Physicist and Mathematician

> Freedom is the right to think, act, speak as your conscience dictates and equal opportunity for all!
> Congresswoman Carolyn B. Maloney NY
> Sponsor Women's Equality Amendment
> Author Rumours of Our Progress are Greatly Exaggerated —

CAROLYN MALONEY
Representative from New York's 13th then 14th District

> INDEPENDENT UK

NIGEL FARAGE
British Politician and Activist

> Freedom means saying out loud what you think.

GARRISON KEILLOR
Radio Host and Author

> FREEDOM IS VIEWING MORE THAN ONE OPINION —

ARMIN DIETER LEHMANN
Hitler's Last Messenger Boy in WWII, and Peace Activist, d.2008

THE FREEDOM CARDS

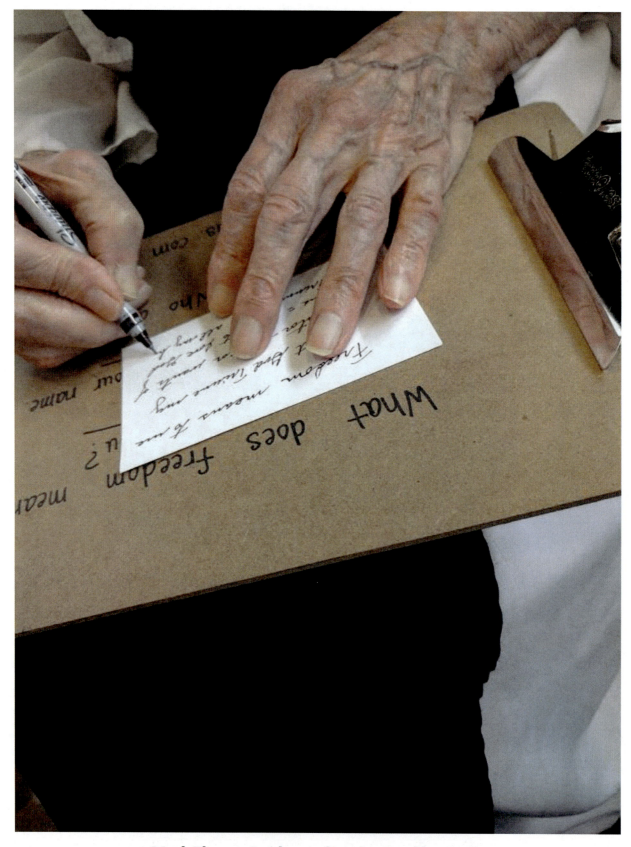

Monk Thomas Smith completes his Freedom Card
at the Monastery of the Holy Spirit in Conyers, Georgia.

THE FREEDOM CARDS

JAMES WATSON
Nobel Prize in Medicine 1962

DIANE WATSON
Representative from California 33rd District 2003-2011

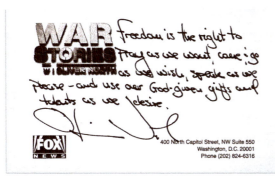

OLIVER NORTH
Lieutenant Colonel Marines, and National Security Advisor

NORM BREYFOGLE
Comic Book Artist, d.2018

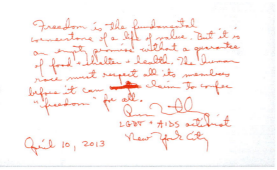

ANN NORTHROP
LGBTQ and AIDS Activist

CHARLES ALBURY
Pilot of *Bockscar*, d.2009

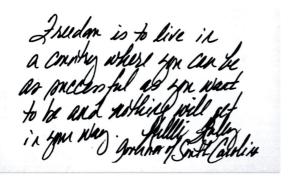

NIKKI HALEY
US Ambassador to the UN 2017-2018

CASEY NEISTAT
Filmmaker and YouTube Creator

THE FREEDOM CARDS

> FREEDOM GIVES YOU THE ABILITY TO FLY AS HIGH AS YOU CAN IMAGINE
>
> *Bob Crippen*

BOB CRIPPEN
Pilot of the First Space Shuttle Mission

> Freedom provides the motivation and opportunity to change your circumstances; to rise above the conditions into which you were born.
>
> *Walter Cunningham*
> Col. USMC-Ret. APOLLO 7

WALT CUNNINGHAM
Apollo 7

> FREEDOM TO ME MEANS WE CAN ALL REACH FOR THE STARS!
>
> *Rhea Seddon*
> NASA ASTRONAUT

RHEA SEDDON
Space Shuttle Astronaut

> To be free in America means that I am free to vote, free to move, free to speak and free to worship Jesus.
>
> *Charlie Duke*
> APOLLO 16

CHARLIE DUKE
Moon Walker, Apollo 16

> I'm free to say what I think, travel where I wish, worship where I please and cast a vote that will be counted!
>
> *Jerry Carr*
> CDR, SKYLAB 4

JERRY CARR
Skylab 4, d.2020

> Freedom is the ability to seek, learn, explore without limits
>
> *Gene Kranz*

GENE KRANZ
NASA Chief Flight Director

> Lets preserve our Freedom!
>
> *V Brand*

VANCE BRAND
Apollo–Soyuz Astronaut

> Freedom allows you to think and express your thoughts without fear.
>
> *F. Fred Gregory*

FREDERICK GREGORY
Space Shuttle Astronaut and Test Pilot

ROBERT MCCALL
Artist

THE FREEDOM CARDS

PAUL RYAN
Speaker of the House 2015-2019

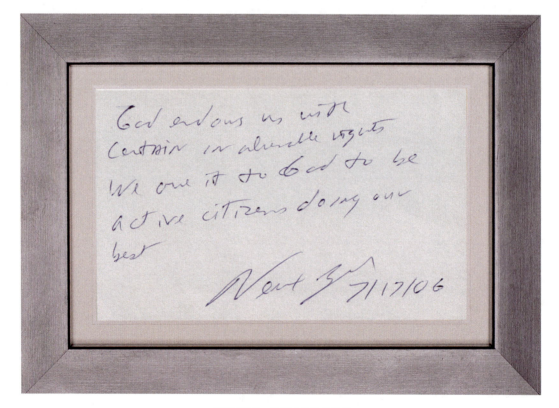

NEWT GINGRICH
Speaker of the House 1995-1999

THE FREEDOM CARDS

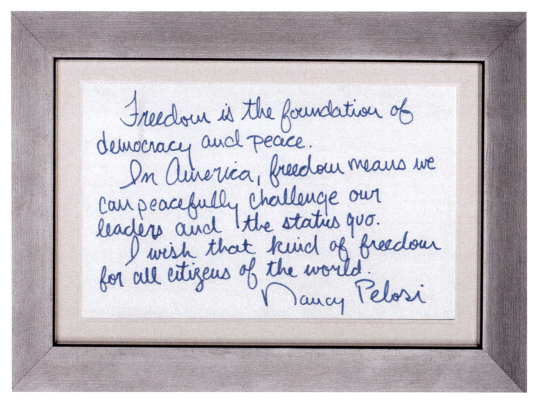

Freedom is the foundation of democracy and peace.
In America, freedom means we can peacefully challenge our leaders and the status quo.
I wish that kind of freedom for all citizens of the world.
Nancy Pelosi

NANCY PELOSI
Speaker of the House 2007-2011, 2019-

The Long Drive to Kansas

Bel Aire, a suburb of Wichita, is situated between Highway 254 and 96 in Kansas's flat middle plains. Residential streets are lined with single-story homes, most painted in neutral colors like sand dune, Mississippi mud, and burnt sienna. The trees lining the city streets are small, newly planted, and with broad green leaves that rustle in hot Midwestern winds.

The Funcheons have lived in Bel Aire for over 15 years in a home not too far from 45th Street, a through road that could take you west to Greenwich, Kansas, or east to I-135. The sun was still shining when I pulled up in front of their home. I kept driving while looking to confirm the house number. I checked it for the third time and stopped the car. I had never met the Funcheons face to face—or even heard their voices. I only knew them through our email and mail conversations. Ms. Funcheon had sent me her picture with her husband and their son Alex a few years before, and now that picture hung in my condo along with a copy of Alex's dog tags. As I walked up their concrete driveway, I saw a sign marking the home—subtle and hidden from the road, a red placard with a gold star.

When I arrived, Ms. Funcheon moved back and forth between a wooden oak table and her kitchen. Her home was decorated with handmade crafts and art—pictures of churches on dirt roads and patterned quilts. Mr. Funcheon sat in a chair next to a desktop computer, which had its monitor boosted with the games Apples to Apples and Trivial Pursuit. The windows were framed with fabric curtains adorned with tiny blue and gold flowers vining from the bottom to the top.

Ms. Funcheon began to serve dinner. The first bowl was full of black beans, the second grated cheddar cheese, then ribbons of lettuce, avocados, and seasoned ground beef. Last was the most crucial ingredient: hot sauce, Alex's favorite. Mr. Funcheon claimed he went through three bottles a week. "He put it on everything!" he told me. I sat with the Funcheons at their table for a few moments before we talked about Alex again—his challenging high school life, why he joined the army.

After dinner, we all got into Mr. Funcheon's gray sedan and began driving through Bel Aire. "This was Alex's high school," Ms. Funcheon said. "Down the road is where he went to Boy Scouts." There were signs for summer festivities and cars for sale. After a 15-minute drive, Mr. Funcheon pulled up in a cemetery and parked a few feet from the road. I waited for the Funcheons to guide me where to go. Mr. Funcheon said, "Here he is." He showed me Alex's gravestone and told me about the service that preceded his burial, the procedure for examining the body after his death, and the pilots that flew him back to Kansas. I listened as Alex's parents narrated stories about him while Mr. Funcheon adjusted the flags by the graveside. Alex was funny and sometimes troubled and always late for things.

After a few moments of silence, the Funcheons began to leave, and I gave Ms. Funcheon an encasing hug. I wanted to say it wasn't fair, but I knew she already knew. I let go and looked over at Mr. Funcheon, and he stretched out his arms for an embrace.

Alex lay six feet below, covered by soil and grass, and cement and wood, and over ten years later, the parades had abated, and the Patriot Guard had driven off. The police cars were back at the precinct, and people who lined the streets had all gone home. Alex was no longer a soldier—he is son and brother—only given to America temporarily and now returned to his mother and father.

Alex's cemetery was so far from everything else. We were alone, away from politics and the news. The scene was tranquil and peaceful, and the crickets buzzed as birds flocked in the blue and pink twilight sky. It was a place I cannot think about without crying. A place where lives end too early and moms are left with holes in their hearts. A place where freedom is not a word anymore. A place in the middle of America, far from the oceans that hit the shores. A place where a boy is laid to rest about a twenty-minute drive from his parents' home. A place you may pass by if you are not looking for it.

KAREN FUNCHEON
Gold-Star Mother

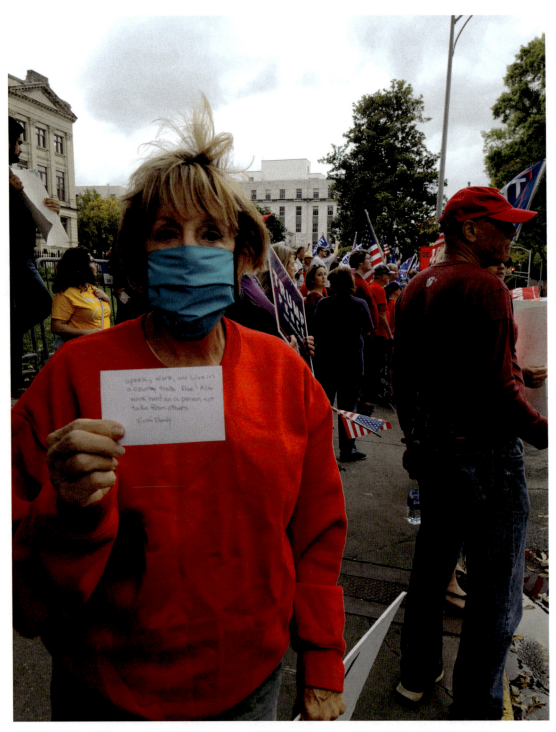

Stop the Steal rally, the Georgia State Capitol. November 7, 2020.
Vicki Dendy: "Speak, Work, and Live in a county that's free!
Also work hard as a person not take from others."

THE FREEDOM CARDS

> Freedom is the very oxygen of the human spirit.
> Joyce Carol Oates

JOYCE CAROL OATES
Writer

> Freedom is to be able to make choices safely
> Isabel Allende

ISABEL ALLENDE
Chilean Writer

> What we talk about when we don't want to talk about justice

JUNOT DIAZ
Writer

> FREEDOM IS INDIVIDUAL AUTONOMY, THE ABILITY TO THINK, BELIEVE, AND EXPRESS ONESELF, TO MAKE CHOICES FOR ONE'S OWN LIFE. THAT MEANS IT IS TIED TO RESPONSIBILITIES TO OTHERS. WE MUST NOT IMPINGE ON OTHERS' FREEDOM, AND MUST ACT POSITIVELY TO REMOVE BARRIERS TO CHOICE.
> PULITZER AND NATIONAL BOOK AWARD-WINNING BIOGRAPHER

T. J. STILES
Biographer

My rental car when I went on The Freedom Road Trip.
Trona Wildrose Rd., California

THE FREEDOM CARDS

"For me, freedom means leading a self-determined life that is based on the basic values of human dignity, justice, and solidarity."
Translated from German

HANS-JOCHEN VOGEL
Mayor of Munich 1960-1972, Mayor of West Berlin 1981, Germany,
and Leader of the German Social Democratic Party from 1987-1991. d.2020

JERRY JEFF WALKER
Singer-Songwriter, d. 2020

PAT THURSTON
Radio Talk Show Host

APOLO ANTON OHNO
Olympic Speed Skater

FRED JOHNSON
Pearl Harbor Veteran, d.2020

THE FREEDOM CARDS

"He whom the Son (Jesus) makes free — shall be free indeed" John 8:36
Jacob DeShazer

JACOB DESHAZER
Doolittle Raider, WWII Veteran, d.2008

THANK GOD THAT WE CONTINUE TO BE ABLE TO LET FREEDOM RING ON A FREE PEOPLE.
Governor John Spellman

JOHN SPELLMAN
Governor of Washington, d.2018

Freedom to me means I can live my life as I choose, so long as I do not break any laws. Without Freedom you really don't live, you survive! God Bless America and Freedom that comes with being an American!
Rick Barry
Basketball Hall of Fame
NBA TOP 50 PLAYER

RICK BARRY
NBA Basketball Player

To the Freedom Project:
For me, freedom is the ability and blessing to choose my path in the direction I discern God's calling to me, while maintaining my love for (and responsibility to) my neighbor.
The Rt. Rev. Gene Robinson
IX Bishop of New Hampshire

GENE ROBINSON
Episcopal Bishop of New Hampshire 2004-2013

Where the Spirit of the Lord is, there is liberty —
Ask our Founding Fathers. Freedom is the liberty to choose what's right
Pat Boone

PAT BOONE
Musician, Singer

Freedom is being able to express that nothing is more important to me than my walk with God.
Mary Costa
2020

MARY COSTA
Opera Singer

Freedom means being able to do what you want, how you want and when you want — as long as you don't block others from their God given freedom.

SCOTT WALKER
Governor of Wisconsin 2011-2019

FREEDOM: 7.10.16
The ability to create my own happiness in life independent of anything or anyone
Freedom is the state in which God intended us to live.

KERRI WALSH JENNINGS
USA Volleyball Player

THE FREEDOM CARDS

What Freedom Means to Me –

To me, freedom means to be able to worship God. It also means being able to tell others about His wonderful love and His Son, Jesus Christ, who died on Calvary's cross for our sins, was raised the third day, and is alive forevermore.

Franklin Graham
President and CEO
Billy Graham Evangelistic Association
Samaritan's Purse

FRANKLIN GRAHAM
Pastor and Activist

Apostolic Nunciature

Freedom is the power, rooted in reason and will, to act or not to act, to do this or that, and so to perform deliberate actions on one's own responsibility. ... Human freedom is a force for growth and maturity in truth and goodness; it attains its perfection when directed toward God, our beatitude. (No. 1731 The Catechism of the Catholic Church)

+ Carlo Maria Viganò
Apostolic Nuncio

CARLO MARIA VIGANÒ
Apostolic Nuncio to the United States, 2011-2016

For me, freedom means the ability to live my life in accordance with the Will of the Lord, without violating fair and just laws consonant with the natural law, and without undue and unreasonable infringement by any government. As Blessed Pope John Paul II remarked, "genuine freedom is the liberty to do what we <u>ought</u>, not whatever we want."

Timothy Michael Cardinal Dolan
Archbishop of New York
April 25, 2013

TIMOTHY DOLAN
Cardinal of New York

THE FREEDOM CARDS

DANIELLE FISHEL
Actress, *Boy Meets World*

HY EISMAN
Cartoonist

ART DONOVAN
NFL Football Player, d.2013

AMY ACUFF
Team USA Track and Field

BENJAMIN FERENCZ
Prosecutor at the Nuremberg Trials

LEON PANETTA
Secretary of Defense 2011-2013, CIA Director 2009-2011

ALEX TREBEK
Host of *Jeopardy*, d.2020

NICHOLAS KATZENBACH
US Attorney General 1965-1966

THE FREEDOM CARDS

Freedom has with it responsibility and duties.
Dan Rather
Journalist
USA

DAN RATHER
Journalist

Freedom is a precious and fragile commodity enjoyed by those willing to protect it.
Robin Olds
B Gen. USAF (Ret)

ROBIN OLDS
WWII and Vietnam War Fighter Pilot, d.2007

Freedom is everything.
Beth Grant ♡
Lucky character actor, trudging the happy road!

BETH GRANT
Actress

Freedom is to be able to have a CHOICE!
Phil Collins
DRUMMER/SINGER

PHIL COLLINS
Musician

Freedom is the blessing that inspired me to fight like hell for the right to fight for my country.
Ben Kuroki

Only Japanese American to bomb Tokyo and Japan mainland in B-29 (28 missions) during WWII.

BEN KUROKI
WWII Veteran, d.2015

FREEDOM IS THE RIGHT (DUTY?) TO RIP ON THE VAIN AND THE POWERFUL.
— S. Pastis
JAN 2016

STEPHAN PASTIS
Cartoonist

Freedom to me meant I could become a professional Woman Baseball player and travel the country.
Joan Berger-Kresl
All American Girls League
Rockford Peaches 1951 & 1954
1954 to 1958 All American Touring Team

JOAN BERGER
Baseball Player in the All-American Girls
Professional Baseball League

Cicero wrote: "Freedom is participation in power."
Freedom requires justice. Without justice freedom cannot flower.
R Nader

RALPH NADER
Activist and Presidential Candidate

Freedom means two interlocking elements:
1. The individual, family or group are free from the coercive power of the state
2. With that freedom, each may pursue — and should pursue — his higher aspirations for the well-being of society.

James Schlesinger
former Sec. of Defense,
Sec. of Energy, and
Director of Central Intelligence

JAMES SCHLESINGER
Secretary of Defense 1973-1975, Secretary of Energy 1977-1979, d.2014

Freedom is the American birthright -- a birthright preserved by generations past who ventured across oceans, stormed beaches, and stood vigilant guard against liberty's enemies. And because of brave servicemen and women serving in places far from home today, we can be assured that future generations of Americans will inherit the same freedom bequeathed to us.

DONALD RUMSFELD
Secretary of Defense 1975-1977, 2001-2006

THE FREEDOM CARDS

> To me "freedom" is "choice"
> my choice of Religion, Education,
> Home, occupation, Political Leaders
> Life Style and even my
> Country all and more are mine
> to choose — Alexander Haig

ALEXANDER HAIG
Secretary of State 1981-1982, d.2014

> Freedom is the ability
> to live your hopes
> — Henry A. Kissinger

HENRY KISSINGER
National Security Advisor 1969-1975, Secretary of State 1973-1977

Protest at Donald Trump's Inauguration
January 20, 2017

Ashes fell from the sky like snow, landing on the heads of the protesters and the helmets of the police standing guard by the burnt skeleton of a black limousine. Most people were staring at their feet or the burning trash cans on K Street. The air smelled like burning plastic, biting my nose and throat. Photographers and reporters bounced person to person with small notepads as they jockeyed for a quote: "Why are you here?" "What do you hope to accomplish?" Then the police moved forward again.

I was on K Street, along with Trump supporters, curious onlookers, protesters, and rioters. We all moved towards the end of the street. Next to me, a photographer stopped for a moment to take a photo and was immediately sprayed with pepper spray. He yelled in agony, "Fuck, fuck, fuck, fuck!" Everyone moved faster.

Protesters dropped their signs and left their messages on the street. The police stopped after their lines encased the burning trash cans. As the photographer rubbed his eyes a few feet away, a protester took a milky substance and sprayed it on his face. Some protesters grabbed broken bricks and hurled them at the police. They hit their round shields and bounced off. It was medieval, like a scene from *Game of Thrones*.

The protesters formed two lines of about 30 people, each facing away from the police. They linked up arms to arms and began chanting, *"The people united will never be defeated,"* and *"These are our streets."*

For a moment, calm ensued. In the bars surrounding the scene, faces were pressed up against the windows. A man wearing a tuxedo peeped through the window three stories up. A group of Trump supporters jeered the protesters, "You lost!" "Get out the billy clubs!" I stood beside that group for a while as one man told another about his tour of duty in Iraq and how he would not let "these folks burn an American flag. I'll stop them." The man next to him wearing a "Make America Great Again" hat nodded in agreement. Every few minutes, a protester would walk by, and a verbal altercation would ensue—sometimes incited by the activist and other times by Trump supporters—and each time it ended the same way, with a phrase like, "They're not worth it."

In 2013, I began contacting people involved in the Syrian Civil War. I used a series of internet ads and online forums. A few people reached out to me. This message came from an individual that wished to remain anonymous.

In 2008 I was skateboarding in Damascus in a huge park called (tishreen park). 2 reporters came to me and asked me a few questions. They were happy to see me skating because they knew a skateboarding could finally be someone who can speak English. He asked me do you have a Facebook account and how do you feel that your government block Facebook ? And other social media ? I was shaking just to hear the question. I was like are you a real reporter or an agent for the government. Because these kind of questions can send you underground for so many years ? After few minutes he gained my trust. And he reordered my answer on a small mp3 recorder. I had dreams that night that they will come and get me just because I talked to an american reporter.

What Im trying to say here is freedom when I can speak to others about my own political views without having nightmares.

Freedom is to hold my camera and take some pictures of a nice street without some stupid armed men come and break my nick.

I never thought what freedom could mean to me. All what happened in 2011 is that I saw we were living like animals. And its time to improve our life that's all.

Freedom is when I open a business in Syria without Assad family come and put their hands on 40% of my projects.

Freedom for me is living in a country under the rules that implied for everyone. Everyone should follow the rule Everyone. That's all my dream is. That's why I wake up every morning and dreaming about going somewhere to Europe or USA.

I'm just an artist I never knew anything in politics. And I don't have the well to do. I just want to have an equal life. To get job opportunity like Assad friends and family do.

I think I talk too much. Sorry man its just I am so heart broken. I cry everyday. I am literally cry like a baby. I'm 23 year old guy who is life is so fucked up (sorry for the words) I don't know what to do anymore. No degree no job no family and no friends. Its like Assad took everything from me just because I asked for some freedom !

ANONYMOUS
Syrian Involved in the Syrian Civil War, 2016

THE FREEDOM CARDS

ERSKINE BOWLES
White House Chief of Staff 1997-1998

> Freedom is Life its own self —

MATTHEW EVERSMANN
Veteran of The Battle of Mogadishu, Black Hawk Down

> Freedom is the end result of countless men and women's actions inspired by a creed or mantra that says "Never shall I fail my comrades." RLTW
> Matthew P. Eversmann
> Task Force Ranger

KEN MORROW
1980 Miracle on Ice Hockey Player

> Freedom allows us to think for ourselves and be accountable for our choices. It forces us to be creative and responsible.
> Ken Morrow
> 1980 'Miracle on Ice'

ALFRED UHRY
Writer

> Freedom is the breath of life
> Alfred Uhry

KELLY BENSIMON
Reality TV Star, *Real House Wives of New York*

> Freedom is the ability to take leaps of faith, never look back, and to go for whatever you want against all odds.
> Kelly Killeen Bensimon
> author, model, Real Housewife of NYC

DAVE BARRY
Writer

> Freedom, to me, means that I can make fun of powerful people, and they can't chop my head off. So far, anyway.
> Dave Barry

TINA LOUISE
Actress, *Gilligan's Island*

> 7/15/06
> Freedom to me means writing what I want, reading what I want, expressing my opinions as I please, living in a democracy and praying that it will bring peace soon.
> Tina Louise

DAVID SCOTT
Representative from Georgia's 13th District

> I defer to the words of Langston Hughes: "O, let my land be a land where Liberty is crowned with no false patriotic wreath, But opportunity is real, and life is free, Equality is in the air we breathe."
> David Scott
> Member of Congress

THE FREEDOM CARDS

> Freedom allows us the opportunity to celebrate our differences and find common ground, with open-mindedness, compassion and humor!
>
> — Bruce R Hornsby

BRUCE HORNSBY
Musician

> Freedom is love because we are freest when we are with those we love most. To affirm humanity's right to freedom is to affirm our love for humanity and life itself.

ANÍBAL ACEVEDO VILÁ
Governor of Puerto Rico 2005–2009

> Freedom is the right to believe as I wish, to live as I wish + to express how I feel without anyone imposing their thoughts on me.
>
> — Joan Rivers

JOAN RIVERS
Actress and Comedian, d.2014

> Economics is all about incentives. And freedom assures that incentives are aligned with the good of all.

ART LAFFER
Economist

> Freedom enables individuals and societies to develop their full potential... in creativity, prosperity, culture, and goodness. It is priceless.
>
> — Barbara H. Franklin
> former U.S. Secretary of Commerce

BARBARA FRANKLIN
Secretary of Commerce 1992–1993

> FREEDOM TO ME MEANS DRAWING MY DAILY CARTOON FOR NEWSPAPERS IN THE U.S. AND AROUND THE WORLD AND CREATE A LITTLE BRIGHTNESS IN THE GLOOM OF DAILY NEWS.
>
> BRAD ANDERSON AND MARMADUKE

BRAD ANDERSON
Cartoonist

> Freedom means doing what I want — or **not** doing something — without the government telling me what to do.
>
> — Ari Fleischer

ARI FLEISCHER
White House Press Secretary 2001–2003

> Freedom is to be yourself in any space without ridicule
>
> — Mayor Monique Owens
> City of Eastpointe, MI

MONIQUE OWENS
Mayor of Eastpointe, Michigan

German Messerschmitt Me 109S, similar to the plane flown by Hugo Broch

National Archives 193711337

THE FREEDOM CARDS

ALFRED REGENITER
German WWII Solider, d.2016

LORIS BALDI
Italian WWII Pilot, d.2016

(Translated from Italian) Freedom means being free to do whatever the law allows us to do.

HUGO BROCH
German WWII Pilot

(Translated from German) What is freedom? Personally, I experienced freedom through "the flight." "Democratic freedom" for us all is essential! "Good that we have it!" With greetings of freedom.

Soldiers prepare to land on the beaches of Normandy during D-Day

National Archives LC-USZ62-92432

> THE CROSS OF FREEDOM IS WITH OUR UNIVERSE
>
> *Jockey Moffat*

JOHN MOFFAT
Scottish WWII Pilot, Credited with Sinking *The Bismarck*, d.2016

> The whole world seeks freedom — from want, from violence, from persecution, from warfare.
>
> Ian C. Hammerton
> MBE, C de G

IAN HAMMERTON
English WWII Officer During D-Day

Freedom is a right to life, liberty, and the pursuit of happiness. Freedom isn't free.

Leandra Lauge
Catholic wife, mother & sidewalk counselor

I sat down to eat a piece of ice cream cake at the dinner table of Erin Duba, and I wasn't five bites in before her friend, Leandra Large, was talking to me about abortion. It wasn't Leandra's fault; I had asked about what she meant by "sidewalk counselor," when I had asked her about what she did. Leandra showed me her phone, and her lock screen was a photo of a child. "I've saved three babies," she said, "and this is one."

Workers hang American flag at Make America Great Again rally in Macon, Georgia.

THE FREEDOM CARDS

> Make America
> Great Again Rally
>
> *Macon, GA, October 16, 2020*

> The right to free speech, Bare Arm, Own A Business, Be safe in our communties, free to worpship, Free to be happy.
>
> *Tynisha Williams*

KESHA WILLIAMS

> to me freedom means the Ability to think on my own and do as I please without Question.
> — cameron screws
> I am A student that belives America is the best Place on Earth.

CAMERON SCREWS

> America
>
> *Kelly Loeffler*

KELLY LOEFFLER
Senator from Georgia 2020-2021

> Freedom = To worship as I wish with no fear
> Tammy Y.

TAMMY Y.

> Freedom means to me that anything that you truly grow up & believe in matters.
> Gracie Y.

GRACIE Y.

> The right to free speech, Bare Arm, Own A Business, Be safe in our communties, free to worpship, Free to be happy.
>
> *Tynisha Williams*

TYNISHA WILLIAMS

> 1. Freedom to me means standing up for what you believe in just like the first amendment says Freedom of speech
> I am Jarvis Atkins

JARVIS ATKINS

THE FREEDOM CARDS

Students Voices

> Freedom is the opening to a ~~good~~ surplus of opportunities
>
> — Kennedy
>
> Student

KENNEDY
High School Student

> Dear Alex
> Freedom is that thing you have that gives you the right to do anything you want... until you get in trouble for it.
>
> — Mills

MILLS
High School Student

> Freedom is the ability to live your life, accomplish your goals, and leave your legacy without fear of persecution.
>
> Nicholas
> Student and aspiring successful person

NICHOLAS
High School Student

> Because I couldn't decide I wrote both...
> ① "Freedom is possessing the knowledge that you will wake up every morning with the power to do what you wish."
> ② "Freedom is what leaves you with no excuse to accomplish your dreams."
>
> — Emma
> Student, Class of 2016

EMMA
High School Student

> I was lucky enough to be born into freedom. My freedom has never been threatened, but if it ever is, I know I will fight for it. I will fight for freedom for myself and others because we are all human, with beating hearts that beat as one and blood flowing through our viens. We all deserve freedom.
>
> — Niki
> Teenage girl

NIKI
High School Student

> ✻ Freedom can be given & taken at any time. Like others Freedom can overwelm you & thats when your no longer free. ✻
>
> Julian
> student [2016]

JULIAN
High School Student

> Freedom is reading. Imersing yourself in a world of newness. Freedom is words, writing, expression. Freedom is literature.
>
> Abeo
> — reader, writer, student

ABEO
High School Student

Note: These cards have been altered to exclude the last names of the students.

THE FREEDOM CARDS

> Freedom means you can buy an ice cream, play in the grass, or cool off in a pool. It is the ability to do the things you want to, and the things you don't. You can go to school, go to work, and pay your taxes. Freedom is to make your own rules.
>
> David
> student, soccer player, paintballer, awsome

DAVID
Middle School Student

> Freedom to me is not being torn down by people who want to be in charge. In America, we can be who we want, when we want, and where we want, without anyone stopping us.
>
> MVPS Student

JON
Middle School Student

> What freedom means to me is being able to paint out my own life.
>
> Kaitlyn
> Student of 2018

KAITLYN
Middle School Student

> To me, freedom is complete equality between different groups, such as race and gender, and equal opportunities.
>
> Robert, a MVPS student

ROBERT
Middle School Student

> "Freedom is the ability to have a mind of your own and make your own desicions."
>
> Brandon
> MVPS Student

BRANDON
Middle School Student

> freedom to me means having the ability to go out of the ordinary to change the world.
>
> —Randi
> (class of 2018) at MVPS

RANDI
Middle School Student

> Freedom is the *happiness, liberty, justice, and rights* that finally were RECIEVED.
>
> —Juliana
> Class of 2018

JULIANA
Middle School Student

> Freedom is how we prosper. Its what we crave. It is our lifeline. It is the only thing that makes us feel truly alive.
>
> —Emma
> Student at Mount Vernon Presbyterian School

EMMA
Middle School Student

Note: These cards have been altered to exclude the last names of the students.

THE FREEDOM CARDS

> Freedom to me means having the basic rights of a human society. The basic rights include the Bill of Rights and the Amendments of America.

> Freedom is when you can achieve your goals w/ no one holding you back.

> Freedom is to me is to be able to be myself.

> To me freedom means having all that you want and taking advantage of it but, not knowing how much you appreciate it until you don't have freedom any more. It's special and a once in a life time opportunity.

> Freedom is having the right to live your life the way you want to. Being able to make choices & come face to face with your own consequences. Freedom is being able to worship who or what you want. Freedom's living.

ANONYMOUS STUDENTS

THE FREEDOM CARDS

> To me, freedom means being able to worship God without being critizied for it; being able to express myself without people ~~stereotyping me~~ labling me; judging because they don't like something about me. It means that I can speak my mind without my parents getting sued for it!

> Freedom means to me means gives us the right to be our self and speak our mind

> Freedom is living by your own guidelines and thoughts

> freedom is the right to do what you want when you want

When I was a senior in high school, students at my school completed cards to contribute to the project.

> "What Freedom Means To Me"
> — Jim L Markham
>
> Being able to act, say, and do whatever one pleases represents the typical view of American Freedom. Our freedom carries with it the responsibility to act, speak, and do in ways that make the American dream of freedom our reality. Freedom does not come cheap. "We the people" are more than a phrase in a document. It means that the continuation of our freedom is our sacred obligation. We are a people blessed with the ability to move between states as we please. It also means that we must be ready to fight for it if necessary. — Jim

JIM MARKHAM
Vietnam Veteran and My High School Principal, d.2019

THE FREEDOM CARDS

DARREN ARONOFSKY
Filmmaker

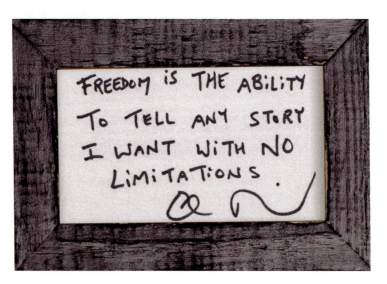

ELI ROTH
Filmmaker

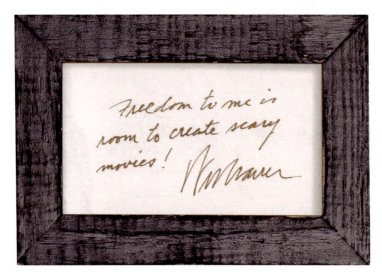

WES CRAVEN
Filmmaker

JIM PHILLIPS
Graphic Artist

White Power Rally Counter-Protest
Stone Mountain Park, DeKalb County, GA,
April 23, 2016

THE FREEDOM CARDS

> *Freedom gives us the vision to see who, how, and where we can help in the world.*
>
> — **Tony Shalhoub**, ACTOR

TONY SHALHOUB
Actor, *Monk*

> "To gain our freedom we should not limit the freedom of others".
>
> — Creed Bratton

CREED BRATTON
Actor, *The Office*

> *Freedom gives me the ability to dream big and know nothing is impossible if your goal is an honorable one.* ♥ *Carol Burnett*

CAROL BURNETT
Actress, *The Carol Burnett Show*

> Freedom is the ultimate gift and expression of our humanity for each other. It is how we say— "I believe in you, I trust you and I wish you a good and fulfilling life". Freedom is the greatest show of respect we can offer another person.
>
> — J. Alexander

JASON ALEXANDER
Actor, *Seinfeld*

> America equals freedom and we should never take that for granted.
>
> — Henry Winkler 2/16/07

HENRY WINKLER
Actor, *Happy Days*

> To say what I think—and to hear what others think, no matter how much we disagree, that's freedom to me. I get to talk—and so do they.
>
> — Alan Alda, ACTOR-WRITER

ALAN ALDA
Actor, *M*A*S*H*

> *Freedom makes me respect America and its military*
>
> — Cybill Shepherd

CYBILL SHEPHERD
Actress, *Cybill*

> Freedom is living without fear. It is opportunity.
>
> — Kevin Nealon, comedian

KEVIN NEALON
Actor and Comedian, *Weeds*

THE FREEDOM CARDS

> Freedom is a state of mind, not freedom from something.
>
> I am a work in progress, in the process of evolving
>
> —Elliott Gould

ELLIOT GOULD
Actor, *Ocean's Eleven*

> Freedom means choice.
> Choice to live where I want.
> Choice to marry who I want.
> Choice to practice my beliefs.
> Choice to speak freely.
>
> —Ernie Hudson
> ACTOR/PLAYWRIGHT
> HUSBAND/FATHER

ERNIE HUDSON
Actor, *Ghostbusters*

> Freedom is our life's work.
>
> —Vera Miles

VERA MILES
Actress, *Psycho*

> Freedom means being able to be anyone, say anything, but that doesn't mean you should just be anybody or do anything you want.

MELISSA JOAN HART
Actress, *Sabrina the Teenage Witch*

> FREEDOM TO ME MEANS BEING ABLE TO PRAY, TRAVEL, VOTE AND SPEAK WHENEVER AND WHERE EVER I AM WITHOUT REGARD TO OUTSIDE FORCES WHICH DO NOT AGREE WITH MY POINT OF VIEW
>
> —Michael Caine

MICHAEL CAINE
Actor, *The Dark Night*

> Freedom is like oxygen, we need it to live.

TIM ALLEN
Actor, *Home Improvement*

> FREEDOM MEANS Everything to me, my Family, my Friends, AND the Animals!!
>
> —Tippi Hedren

TIPPI HEDREN
Actress, *The Birds*

> FREEDOM IS: EVERYTHING.

JON HAMM
Actor, *Madmen*

THE FREEDOM CARDS

DAVID KOECHNER
Actor, *The Office*

JOANNA BARNES
Actress, *The Parent Trap*

BILLY CRYSTAL
Actor, *Monsters Inc.*

FLORENCE HENDERSON
Actress, *The Brady Bunch*

MARTIN SHEEN
Actor, *The West Wing*

GARY BUSEY
Actor, *Lethal Weapon*

SILAS HATHAWAY
Actor, Charlie Chaplin's *The Kid*, Silent Movie Era, WWII Veteran

BAM MARGERA
TV Personality, *Jackass*

158

THE FREEDOM CARDS

> JOY IS IN FREEDOM;
> SERVING GOOD; ITS
> PERFECT EXPRESSION
> SAM WATERSTON.

SAM WATERSTON
Actor, *Law and Order*

> The most important freedom is the one that allows for the obtaining and disseminating of the truth. — Alec Baldwin

ALEC BALDWIN
Actor, *30 Rock*

> FREEDOM FOR ME IS LIVING IN THIS GREAT COUNTRY. BUT WE MUST PLAY BY THE RULES OF GOD & LAND.
> Tab Hunter
> ACTOR, WRITER, PRODUCER

TAB HUNTER
Actor, d.2018

> Freedom means that I get to choose what's right for me. — Jorge

JORGE GARCIA
Actor, *Lost*

> Then you will know the truth and the TRUTH will set you FREE. John 8:32
> Love, Ann B. Davis

ANN DAVIS
Actress, *The Brady Bunch*

> We all hail and cherish freedom. To abuse it is criminal. — Adam West

ADAM WEST
Actor, *Batman*, d.2017

> FREEDOM
> THE FANTASTIC RESULT OF A TOLERANT AND COMPASSIONATE SOCIETY!
> ACTRESS
> HOLLYWOOD, CALIFORNIA

BETTY JAMES
Actress

> Only in FREEDOM can we explore our full potential intellectually, artistically, and psychologically. — Barbara Feldon

BARBARA FELDON
Actress, *Get Smart*

THE FREEDOM CARDS

> Freedom means having the ability to maximize my God given talents for the betterment of me & my family without government interference.
>
> Cathy Purswell

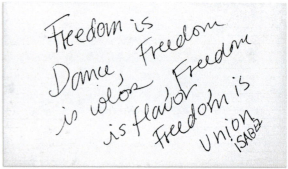

CATHY PURSWELL

Republican Victory Party, Buckhead, GA

> Freedom is Dance, Freedom is color, Freedom is flavor, Freedom is Union.
>
> ISABEL

ISABEL

Campaigner at the corner of Piedmont and Peachtree

> Freedom is the peace that comes knowing you have made the best choices possible, using your God-given gifts. It is sitting comfortably with those choices, void of regret or remorse.
>
> Dennise K. Peagler

DENNISE PEAGLER

Early Voter

> Freedom is having the means to control the way you want to live, the ability to pursue the lifestyle and goals you want to live, and to be responsible and accountable for the outcomes you achieve.

ANDREW QUINN

Voter

160

THE FREEDOM CARDS

Election Day 2016

Freedom to me is for Americans to be able to assert their First Amendment rights as constitutionally allowed. Freedom equals to Liberty
Brad Carver

BRAD CARVER
Campaigner at the Corner of Piedmont and Peachtree

FREEDOM IS...
OUR future as we CONTINUE to elect those who have not long known freedom.

CALLAN WELLS
Voter

Freedom is the right to be an independent person who respects the rights of others. Free to love God and be a witness in speech & actions

DAVID ELLISON
Voter

Freedom means responsibility. We must all perform our civil duty in order to keep our freedom and work to make our dreams come true.
Shawn Wilson

SHAWN WILSON
Voter

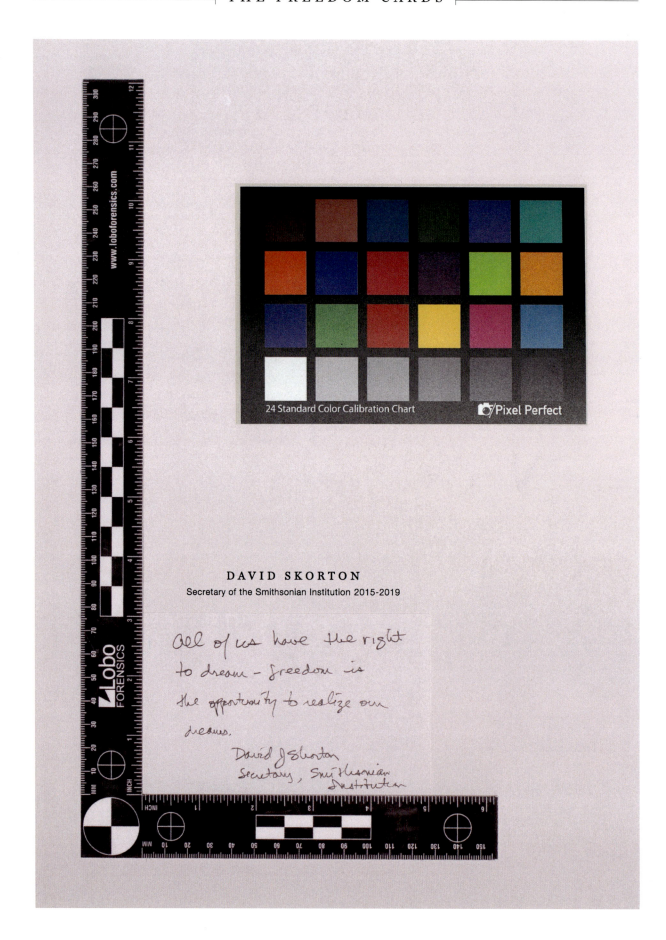

DAVID SKORTON

Secretary of the Smithsonian Institution 2015-2019

All of us have the right to dream — freedom is the opportunity to realize our dreams.

David J Skorton
Secretary, Smithsonian Institution

THE FREEDOM CARDS

> To me, freedom means that you should be able to do what you want with your life, so long as you do not do any harm to anyone else.
>
> *John Gurdon*

SIR JOHN GURDON
Nobel Prize in Medicine 2012

> Freedom empowers us to seek and achieve one's dreams and ambitions. Being free also provides us with an irrevocable right to question, seek answers and to publicise the findings of these investigations.
>
> *Paul Berg, Nobel Laureate Chemistry, 1980*

PAUL BERG
Nobel Prize in Chemistry 1980

> To me, freedom is the right to be wrong. It is the right to be in the minority and to still enjoy the same liberties as those in the majority.
>
> *Michael S Brown, Nobel Prize in Medicine 1985*

MICHAEL BROWN
Nobel Prize in Medicine 1985

> Freedom is being able to pursue what you believe is right, good and beautiful, with respect for every person, but no reason to fear anyone.
>
> *Samantha Cristoforetti, Astronaut of the European Space Agency of Italian Nationality*

SAMANTHA CRISTOFORETTI
Astronaut and Engineer

> Freedom encourages creativity, allowing individuals to break with standardized thought and behavior.
>
> *Chas. H. Townes*
>
> March 19, '07

CHARLES TOWNES
Nobel Prize in Physics 1964, d.2015

> Freedom is protection from slavery or oppression. It is precious, but it is not absolute, and it is not synonymous with licence, for it entails self-discipline, responsibility, and accountability.
>
> *Michael E. DeBakey, M.D.*
> Chancellor Emeritus
> Baylor College of Medicine
> Director, DeBakey Heart Center

MICHAEL DEBAKEY
Surgeon, d.2008

> 12/22/06
> Freedom will come about when we become a caring world. A caring world will come about when we stop the stupidity and end wars. When the money spent on wars is used to provide all people with food, health care, and a safe environment we will have a caring world and be free.
>
> *Henry J Heimlich*

HENRY HEIMLICH
Surgeon, Developer of the Heimlich Maneuver, d.2016

> 11-14-06
> Freedom means the ability to make and fulfill decisions vital to myself and my family –
>
> *Denton A. Cooley MD*

DENTON COOLEY
Surgeon, d.2016

> Where there is equal access and equal opportunity, freedom means an open door to develop talents through education and meaningful performance that maintains our countries strengths and values.
>
> Charles E. McGee, Col USAF (Ret.)
> Tuskegee Airman

CHARLES MCGEE
Tuskegee Airmen

Major James A. Ellison reviews first class of Tuskegee Airmen

US Air Force photo, 1941

THE FREEDOM CARDS

Women's March, Washington, D.C.

Jan 21, 2017

Freedom means liberty and justice for all through government by the people, with equal protection under law!

Sarah Rice Fox

a multilingual educator from San Diego, California

SARAH RICE FOX

Ideally, freedom means equality. Freedom means determination & spirit.

DCurley

DIXIE CURLEY

DIXIE CURLEY

Over my body

Deb Lantz

DEB LANTZ

I am my own and make my own decisions

Jessica Curley

Daughter, Sister, Aunt, Woman

JESSICA CURLEY

Freedom to me is the right of everyone to pursue love, peace, the pursuit to live, work, receive an education, without interruption or hate or discrimination

Cindy Curley
Georgia

CINDY CURLEY

Freedom means never having to be afraid of WHO YOU ARE.

—Katie Kinka ("Modern Rosie")

KATIE KINKA

---

*Kathy from Cape Cod
Justice for all
Intelligent collaboration*

KATHY

Women's March on Washington, January 19, 2017, Washington, D.C.

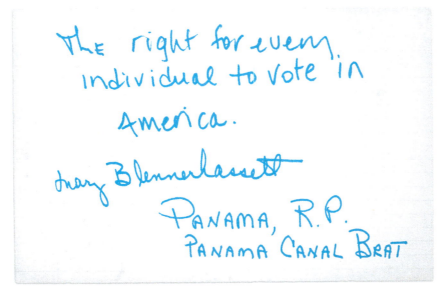

The right for every individual to vote in America.

Mary Blennerhassett
Panama, R.P.
Panama Canal Brat

MARY BLENNERHASSETT

THE FREEDOM CARDS

> Freedom, for me is:
> Never having to explain myself!
> *Rita Moreno*

RITA MORENO
Actress and Singer

> freedom to me means I am able to pursue my dreams as well as encourage my daughter and other girls to do and be whatever they want to be.
> (UFC Fighter) *Montana De La Rosa*

MONTANA DE LA ROSA
Mixed Martial Artist

> Freedom to me is to be able to think, do, and say anything I want as long as I stay within the law.
> *Eddie Robinson*

EDDIE ROBINSON
Oldest Living Former Baseball Player

> Freedom has the ability to make your own choices without government running your life.
> *Corey Lewandowski*

COREY LEWANDOWSKI
Donald Trump Campaign Manager 2015-2016

> Freedom is the very essence of America.
> Governor John Hoeven
> North Dakota

JOHN HOEVEN
Governor of North Dakota 2000-2010,
Current Senator from North Dakota

> Freedom means Life!
> *Meta H Doran*
> Am a holocaust survivor and without freedom there would not be a life.

META DORAN
Holocaust Survivor, d.2019

> Freedom's just another word For nothing left to lose
> *Kris Kristofferson*

KRIS KRISTOFFERSON
Singer and Songwriter

> Freedom is a necessity, like air + water.
> *Alison Lurie*

ALISON LURIE
Writer

THE FREEDOM CARDS

> Freedom is the privilege to make your own choices.
> Kerri Strug
> Olympic Gold medal gymnast 1996

KERRI STRUG
Olympic Gymnast

> Freedom is my right to believe in what and who I want to!

ANNALEIGH ASHFORD
Actress, Singer

> Freedom means no one is taking care of you.

ROBERT BALLARD
Explorer and Oceanographer

> To me, freedom is the life blood of democracy
> Ted Sorensen

TED SORENSEN
John F. Kennedy's Speech Writer and Advisor, d.2010

> Freedom — December 2013
> "Power to seek the truth"
> Neil Tyson

NEIL DEGRASSE TYSON
Astronomer

> MY IDEA OF FREEDOM IS SMOKING A FAT JOINT ON THE CAPITOL STEPS WHILE STANDING NEXT TO CAPITOL POLICE TO SAY FUCK A CORRUPT GOVERNMENT AND THE CORPORATE OLIGARCHY THEY CREATED WITHOUT GETTING ARRESTED.... OH WAIT º
> — MATT HORNING

MATT HORNING
Protester Charged in Connection with the January 6 Riot at the Capitol

> Freedom is something we all want. But, surprisingly, seldom have
> Edgar Wayburn

EDGAR WAYBURN
Environmentalist, d.2010

> Freedom is complex and personal. Do I stand with the singer or the censor? The rapist or the raped? And at what risk? My daily choices introduce me to freedom — and to myself.
> Holly Near
> 2014

HOLLY NEAR
Singer-Songwriter, Activist

July 15, 1976

Library of Congress, Photo number 1633553

THE FREEDOM CARDS

Freedom is the essence of democracy and human dignity —

J Carter

JIMMY CARTER
39th President 1977-1981

Everything

Wm Mondale

WALTER MONDALE
Vice President 1977-1981, Democratic Nominee for President 1984

John McCain after being released from a North Vietnam POW Camp

National Archives, 1973, 1633553

THE FREEDOM CARDS

The service of every past and present American soldier has helped guarantee the freedom we enjoy today.

— John McCain

JOHN MCCAIN
Vietnam Veteran, Senator from Arizona 1987-2018, d.2018

Freedom to me means the ability to be deeply and actively involved in politics and public service in my community and in my country without fear or favor. — Mike Dukakis

MICHAEL DUKAKIS
Governor of Massachusetts 1975-1979, 1983-1991

Freedom is the power to break down barriers. This is not only our right, it is our responsibility.

— Geraldine Ferraro
First & only woman to run for Vice President (1984)

GERALDINE FERRARO
Representative from New York's 9th 1979-1985, d.2011

Quote:

"Freedom is responsibility. It is living our lives the way we choose while respecting the rights of others to do the same, and who do the same for us. While it is rooted in basic laws, it is more importantly anchored in a tradition of responsibility, mutual respect and duty that must accompany freedom in order for it to thrive. When expressed appropriately, and defended from threat or coercion or malice, freedom is the principle that elevates humanity and allows us to fulfill our tremendous promise. It does not guarantee individual results, but it provides the only foundation upon which they can possibly be achieved."

— Bob Dole

BOB DOLE
Senator from Kansas 1969-1996

FREEDOM

Freedom is what the human spirit longs for! It's one of the few things in life that's worth both living and dying for — as our brave women & men in uniform know.

— Governor Sarah Palin

SARAH PALIN
Governor of Alaska 2006-2009

THE FREEDOM CARDS

> America is great because America is free. If we lose our freedom, we lose our greatness —
> — Dan Quayle 44th/VP

DAN QUAYLE
Vice President 1989-1993

America is a great nation whose citizens enjoy an abundance of freedom and opportunity. The ability of Americans to speak their minds about any issue, no matter how controversial or unpopular, is the defining freedom of this country. This freedom protects all our other freedoms, and undermining it would threaten all others.

All the best to you.

Sincerely,

Bill Clinton

BILL CLINTON
President 1993-2001

Black Lives Matter Protest, Atlanta, GA, June 1, 2020

"Freedom means equality. Freedom means peace. Freedom means harmony."
—Jake (Left)

THE FREEDOM CARDS

> Freedom means being, sleeping, eating, and doing whatever you want without fear.
>
> — Bill McCrary

BILL MCCRARY
Negro League Player 1946-1947, d.2018

> Freedom = Chance 2 Love Everything Around You! Don't Abuse it!
>
> — Jeff Hardy

JEFF HARDY
Professional Wrestler

> Freedom to me means the right and ability of each person to reach their full potential as a human being.
>
> — Mackenzie Dern, UFC Fighter

MACKENZIE DERN
UFC Fighter

> Freedom is the right to do and say whatever I wish, unfettered by an onerous government or corrupt private interests.
>
> — James Risen, Pulitzer Prize winning investigative reporter

JAMES RISEN
Journalist

> Freedom to me is believing in the innovation, life and leadership of Black girls.
>
> — Joanne Smith, Founder/CEO

JOANNE N. SMITH
Social Worker and Founder of Girls for Gender Equity

> Freedom is to allow you to do as you wish and reach your goals
>
> — Meyer Steinberg, Chem. Engr. on Manhattan Project, 7/21/2020

MEYER STEINBERG
Chemical Engineer on the Manhattan Project

> Freedom is the ability to live, love, work, and worship as you see fit without interference from other people or governments.
>
> — Trent Lott

TRENT LOTT
Senator from Mississippi 1989-2007

> Alex,
>
> Freedom is the ability to be who you are.
>
> — Linda M. Harrison, June 26, 2020

LINDA HARRISON
Actress

Free Joint Protest, January 18, 2017, Washington, D.C.

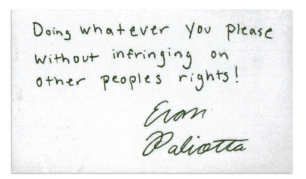

EVAN PALIOTTA

THE FREEDOM CARDS

The IAIA Museum of Contemporary Native Arts, Santa Fe, New Mexico

> Freedom means to be able to exhibit challenging, thought provoking, cutting edge art; and to give artists, who are often overlooked by the mainstream art world, a voice.
>
> Manuela Well-Off-Man
>
> chief curator, IAIA Museum of Contemporary Native Arts

MANUELA WELL-OFF-MAN
Curator of the IAIA Museum of Contemporary Native Arts

The Freedom Road Trip
Summer 2017

THE FREEDOM CARDS

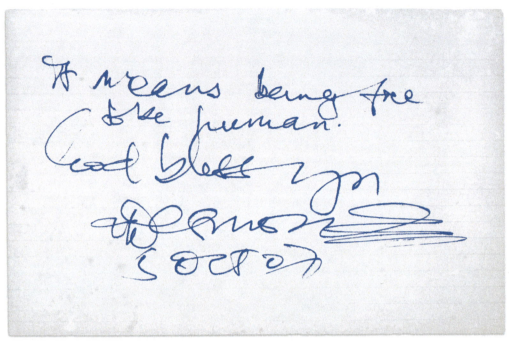

It means being free to be human.
God bless you
+D Mpilo Tutu
(5 Oct 07)

ARCHBISHOP DESMOND TUTU
South African Anti-Apartheid Activist, Nobel Peace Prize 1984

Freedom is empowerment towards the right to make legitimate choices and pursue legitimate goals with minimum and reasonable constraint by any external authority.

FW de Klerk

FW DE KLERK
Former President of South Africa

FW DE KLERK
President of South Africa 1989-1994, Nobel Peace Prize 1993

> Freedom for me is the love of Mother Earth. Freedom for me is working to set others free. Freedom for me knowing that each person I educate in the techniques of non-violence will educate others, and then, one day war will be obsolete! That's freedom for me!

BETTY WILLIAMS
Peace Activist, Nobel Peace Prize 1976, d.2020

> An open society and the rule of law are essential for any country that aspires to be prosperous and free.
> I am content to rely on the freedoms we have built up, step by step through the common law and the British empirical tradition, capable of modification and change through our flexible "constitution".
> DAVID TRIMBLE

DAVID TRIMBLE
Minister of North Ireland 1998-2002, Nobel Peace Prize 1998

THE FREEDOM CARDS

"Freedom," like many words, Things to different people. may mean such an overpopulated end of the human race. are free to speak, we may survive!

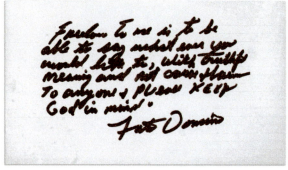

FATS DOMINO
Jazz Pianist, d.2017

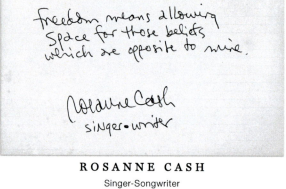

ROSANNE CASH
Singer-Songwriter

CYNDI LAUPER
Singer and Songwriter

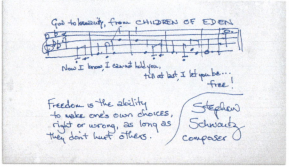

STEPHEN SCHWARTZ
Composer and Lyricist

THE FREEDOM CARDS

means many different
the freedom to have babies
planet that it brings the
But MLK showed us that if we
old Pete Seeger

Mar. 21, 2013

PETE SEEGER
Folk Musician, d.2014

Freedom is having the privilege of playing concerts for people without being afraid — where everyone can truly enjoy themselves both onstage and off.
Sir George Shearing, Jazz pianist

GEORGE SHEARING
Jazz Pianist, d.2011

To be free is to have truth allowed to flourish and grow in mind and spirit and soul.
Dave Brubeck

DAVE BRUBECK
Jazz Pianist, d.2012

Freedom is the independence, flexibility, knowledge, + money, to do the things I desire.
country music hall of famer

RONNIE MILSAP
Country Music Singer

Freedom is our God-given right to BE a Blessing & RECEIVE Blessings, defined by being uniquely ourselves, allowing others to do the same.
· Lev 19:18 · Luke 6:31
· Matt 7:12

DEANA CARTER
Singer and Songwriter

THE FREEDOM CARDS

RABBI ERWIN SCHILD
Canadian Rabbi

Freedom means to have the choice to participate in society: to lead, to devote, or to withdraw and be left alone. Freedom is contingent on everyone else enjoying the same opportunities. The individual is free only in a free society governed by rules that protect, enhance & promote freedom for all.
Growing up in Nazi Germany, I experienced the very opposite of freedom and learned to treasure the life in a free society and to stand on guard for freedom. — Rabbi Erwin Schild

HERMAN CAIN
Candidate for President and Talk Radio Show Host, d.2020

Freedom is the ability to determine your own success or failure or mediocrity.

JOSEPH GALLOWAY
Journalist

I have lived & worked in countries where there was No Freedom! The freedom to speak, to write, to assemble, to worship is precious and fragile.
— Joseph L. Galloway, Journalist & Author

L. PAUL BREMER
American Diplomat

It is an honor to join in your noble project of recognizing the most basic American value — freedom.
— Ambassador L Paul Bremer

JAMES CHRISTY
Astronomer and Discover of Pluto's Moon Charon

Freedom comes from sceptical thinking about what really is true.
— James W. Christy

HANNAH KEARNEY
Olympic Gold Medalist

Freedom is the ability to pursue your dreams.
— Hannah Kearney
Olympic gold medalist, mogul skiing

WILLIAM AYERS
Former Member of the Weather Underground and Professor

Freedom — the act of naming the obstacles to our full humanity and then joining hands to breach those barriers — relies on imagination, that "slow fuse of possibility," to illuminate a world that could be or should be, but is not yet. — William Ayers, teacher

TOMMY CHONG
Actor

Freedom to me? Means — You can try and be anyone you want... and it's all right to fail... We have the freedom to fail and still play the game.

THE FREEDOM CARDS

"FREEDOM" IS MY FAVORITE PART OF LIVING IN A LIBERAL DEMOCRACY BUT ONLY MY 3RD FAVORITE WHAM! SINGLE. ("CARELESS WHISPER" AND "WHAM RAP!" ARE BETTER IMHO.)

Ken Jennings
74-TIME JEOPARDY! CHAMP

KEN JENNINGS
Jeopardy Campion

Freedom is the world's greatest supernatural resource.

Joseph M. Arpaio
Sheriff, Maricopa County
Arizona

JOE ARPAIO
Sheriff of Maricopa County 1993–2017

Freedom is the most precious gift our wonderful forefathers have bestowed upon us.

Severin Fayerman

SEVERIN FAYERMAN
Holocaust Survivor, d. 2015

Freedom is one of the great gifts of God! It is our job to keep it.

Irlene Mandrell

IRLENE MANDRELL
Actress

FREEDOM IS THE Ability to be you AND the Responsibility to HAVE COMMON SENSE AND THE CAPABILITY OF KNOWING RIGHT.

Capt. *Rich Phillips*
U.S. SEAMAN

RICHARD PHILLIPS
Captain of *MV Maersk Alabama* During Somali Pirates Attack

Freedom is the ability to Become whatever We want to become. It's our Responsibility to Achieve the Highest Goals We set, to be as Successful as We can be, allowing GOD to lead us through.

Kurt Angle

KURT ANGLE
Professional Wrestler

For me, Freedom is the ability to do what each of us wants to pursue happiness here on Earth; it highlights the opportunities for each of us to be responsible for our own actions and to leave the world better than we found it.

— *Bill Nye*

BILL NYE
Science Guy

Freedom is For all

Scotty Bowman

SCOTTY BOWMAN
Former NHL Coach

THE FREEDOM CARDS

> It's a great thing to be free, free of anything - speech, religion and thought.
>
> *Maurice Starkey*

MAURICE STARKEY
WWI Veteran, d.2006

> Freedom is the right to make my choice of what to think and do.
>
> Theodore "Dutch" Van Kirk
> Navigator Enola Gay
> Hiroshima 6 Aug 1945

THEODORE VAN KIRK
Navigator of the Enola Gay, d.2014

> - Freedom is being An American!
> - Freedom is having the means to make your own Decisions that decide your own Destiny!
> - Freedom is what we see everyday we wake up. It's the view of what so many service men + women have sacrificed for!

DAKOTA MEYER
Medal of Honor Afghanistan

> Freedom is the ability to live actively and spontaneously without harming others or nature, deeply knowing that an injustice anywhere is a threat to justice everywhere. It takes corrective responsibility when harms from one's actions are made known.
>
> — S. Brian Willson, Viet Nam Veteran, trained lawyer, political activist, and author
> S. Brian Willson Feb 23, 2014

S. BRIAN WILSON
Veteran and Peace Activist

> Freedom for Me is
> 1. Worship where and who I want
> 2. Speak your mind
> 3. Honor our Military and Veterans
>
> GOD Bless America
> Matt Dillon
> LZ XRay, Ia Drang Vietnam 1965

MATT DILLON
Vietnam Veteran

> Freedom to me is being able to speak about what you want, do what you want, be what you want, eat what you want, live where you want, love & like who you want, study what you want, think what you want, feel what you want, go where you want, work where you want, have the religion you want with minimal individual restrictions
>
> Mary Blanchard Bowe
> Vietnam '68-'69
> Donut Dollie

MARY BLANCHARD BOWE
Vietnam War Donut Dollie

> WHAT DOES FREEDOM MEAN TO ME?
>
> FREEDOM IS WHAT OUR CONSTITUTION GIVES TO ALL OF US; AN OPPORTUNITY TO ... "secure the blessings of liberty to ourselves and our posterity..." WHAT A GREAT NATION WE HAVE.
>
> John P. Abizaid
> GEN, USA
> FORMER COMMANDER CENTCOM

JOHN ABIZAID
Commander of CENTCOM 2003-2007

> Freedom is now free but must be earned and received thru hard work and sacrifice.
>
> Col Walt Watson

WALT WATSON
SR-71 Blackbird Pilot

THE FREEDOM CARDS

> Douglas S. Canning
> 1st Lt. 339th Fighter Sqdr.
> Yamamoto Mission Pilot
> 18 April 1943
>
> Freedom in the United States is the ability to go where you want and do what you want as long as it is within the law. DSC

DOUG CANNING
WWII Veteran, d.2016

> Freedom is being able to walk freely down the street without fear.
>
> Bernice "Bee" Falk Hayden
> a WWII veteran who served as a Women Airforce Service Pilot (WASP)

BERNICE FALK HAYDEN
WWII WASP

> Freedom is the God given right to shape our own pathway to our personal destination.
>
> Gail S Halvorsen
> Col USAF (Ret)
> The Berlin Candy Bomber - Pilot - Aeronautical Engineer - Space Program

GAIL HALVORSEN
Berlin Airlift Pilot

> FREEDOM IS THE ABSENCE OF BONDAGE!
>
> PAUL LONGGREAR
> Col USSF
> Ret

PAUL LONGGREAR
Vietnam Veteran

> FREEDOM SHOULD BE VALUED & APPRECIATED, AS IT WAS BOUGHT WITH THE BLOOD OF SERVICE MEN & WOMEN WHO LOVED THEIR COUNTRY
>
> Howard E Wasdin
> • DOCTOR
> • AUTHOR
> • FORMER SEAL TEAM III

HOWARD WASDIN
Navy Seal Team Six

> To me freedom is being able to live in a world at peace. Not all people need to have the same belief but must show respect to one another
>
> Forrest L. Guth
> Co. E, 506 P.I.R., 101 A/B

FORREST GUTH
WWII Veteran and Band of Brothers, d.2009

> Before I can talk about Freedom I have to be free
> As a Black man in America I am not "FREE".
>
> Edgar V. Lewis
> Lt Col. Edgar Lewis
> AH. Chpt. Tuskegee Airmen

EDGAR LEWIS
Tuskegee Airmen, d.2020

> Freedom is the most important human condition required for the fullest development. I fought in WWII, as a fighter pilot, for the freedom of my country, my family, myself and all the people of the world, including the people of my enemies.
>
> Archie F. Maltbie
> Lt. Col. USAF Retired

ARCHIE MALTBIE
WWII Veteran, Band of Brothers, d.2018

On July 11, 2016, Black Lives Matter protesters gathered outside of the Governor's Mansion in Atlanta, GA. They chanted long into the night, accompanied by a pounding drum beat.

"No Justice, No Peace."
"No Justice, No Peace."
"No Justice, No Peace."

Demonstrator Lorean La'Lee Hargo:
"United! Love and Justice."

> *America is free and we must enjoy our freedom by protecting it.*
>
> —Arnold Palmer

ARNOLD PALMER
Professional Golfer, d.2016

= THE FREEDOM CARDS =

What freedom means to me.

To me, Freedom is living a life of purpose, despite the challenges one may face.

Rachel Robinson; Founder of the Jackie Robinson Foundation and wife of the barrier breaking ball player

RACHEL ROBINSON
Activist, Wife of Jackie Robinson

Freedom means allowing yourself to be kind, even though there are so many other options.

REBECCA LOBO
WNBA 1997-2003, Team USA

Freedom is God's gracious gift that makes us His precious children. It is our responsibility to defend that gift always.

Coach of World Champion Baltimore Ravens

JOHN HARBAUGH
Head Coach of the Baltimore Ravens

FREEDOM IS THE ABILITY TO DREAM AND TO PURSUE YOUR DREAM!

MIKE KRZYZEWSKI
Duke Men's Basketball Team Coach

FREEDOM IS THE POWER OF CHOICE. YOU HAVE THE ABILITY TO CHOOSE YOUR OWN PATH. IT GIVES YOU THE ABILITY TO, AS MY MOTHER USED TO SAY, "DREAM BEYOND YOUR SURROUNDINGS!"

JOHN CALIPARI
University of Kentucky Men's Basketball Coach

freedom is the power to act, speak, or think without hindrance or restraint

Bill Belichick NE Patriots

BILL BELICHICK
General Manger and Head Coach of the New England Patriots

Freedom is having a choice. It allows anyone to choose how to be, how to think... anything. The freedom to choose gives us the opportunity to learn & grow through our choices.

SOFTBALL PLAYER- OLYMPIC GOLD ('04) & SILVER ('08) MEDALIST

CAT OSTERMAN
Team USA Softball 2004, 2008, 2020

191

Ralph Williams was the first person to ever send an unsolicited card. I received it in 2007 after an article about the project was printed in my local paper. When I looked him up to put his card in the book, his obituary was the first result. He died not too long ago.

> THE RIGHT TO LIFE, LIBERTY AND FREEDOM TO PURSUE HAPPINESS IN ANY WAY UNLESS ONE IS INJURIOUS TO ANOTHER PERSON.

RALPH D. WILLIAMS
School Principal, d.2018

THE FREEDOM CARDS

DAVID WILHELM
WWII Veteran, ACE Fighter Pilot, d.2018

> With No Freedom; you are not living.
>
> David Wilhelm
>
> Cowboy Ace WWII; Flying fighters was Freedom

JODI RELL
Governor of Connecticut 2004-2011

> Freedom means being able to read any book I choose, listen to music I like, sit on a park bench without fear — and so much more. Freedom means living in America!

RICHARD SIMMONS
Fitness Mogul

> Freedom For Me is Speaking My Mind. Sharing What I Know. and Touching The Hearts of Others.
>
> Love, Richard Simmons

DENNIS BANKS
American Indian Movement Activist, d.2018

> THE RIGHT TO BE WHO WE WERE BORN, FREE TO FOLLOW OUR OWN BELIEFS, OUR OWN SPIRITUAL PATH, OUR OWN LANGUAGE, SONGS, UNDERSTANDINGS! TO BELIEVE IN MOTHER EARTH ≠ OUR OWN CREATOR.
>
> DENNIS BANKS OJIBWAH MAN, Leech Lake Reservation, AMERICAN INDIAN MOVEMENT.

DANIEL ELLSBERG
Leaker of the Pentagon Papers, Activist

> 12-30-13
>
> Freedom involves the right and the ability to say what you believe, to tell the truth that others need to know, even if it's "secret." (This my total courage)
>
> Dan Ellsberg

KARL ROVE
Political Consultant

> Freedom means the right to chart a course for one's life, independent of the dictates of government, except for those limited rules necessary to protect the rights of others.
>
> Karl Rove

COLIN McGINN
Philosopher

> 1. Freedom is the ability to say to people what they do not want to hear
> 2. Freedom is the ability to say what most people find repellent
> 3. Freedom is toleration of the outrageous
>
> C. McGinn
> COLIN McGINN
> PHILOSOPHER

BOB BARKER
TV Show Host and Activist

> FREEDOM ALLOWS US TO MAKE OUR OWN DECISIONS IN LIFE.
>
> Bob Barker
> TELEVISION HOST & ANIMAL RIGHTS ACTIVIST, 2014

THE FREEDOM CARDS

> I can think of no better expression of Freedom than the American Bill of Rights codifying individual rights to health, wealth and the pursuit of happiness taking into account the rights of others.
> — Vinton G. Cerf

VINTON CERF
Internet Engineer

> Freedom means I have the opportunity to live as I like and worship God freely —
> Mike Huckabee, candidate for President of the United States

MIKE HUCKABEE
Governor of Arkansas 1996-2007

> FREEDOM ALLOWS YOU TO CALL OUT THE BAD, THE WRONG, THE AWFUL — AND PERHAPS CHANGE IT. FREEDOM IS WHY THE CIVIL RIGHTS ACT OF 1964 WAS SIGNED INTO LAW, AGAINST THE WISHES OF THEN SENATOR OF GEORGIA RICHARD RUSSELL. RUSSELL HAD THE FREEDOM TO BE A BIGOT, LIKE MARCO RUBIO. FREEDOM, REAL FREEDOM THAT IS — REQUIRES MORAL STRENGTH. DO YOU HAVE IT? — NEVER STOP ASKING. — H. ROLLINS

HENRY ROLLINS
Singer-Songwriter, Activist

> FREEDOM is being allowed to follow your dreams —
> JIM DAVIS
> *(AND THE ICE CREAM TRUCK!)*

JIM DAVIS
Cartoonist

> Freedom gives us peace & prosperity. It happens when the government is restrained.
> Ron Paul

RON PAUL
Representative from Texas 1976-1977, 1979-1985, 1997-20

> To me "FREEDOM" MEANS EQUAL OPPORTUNITY FOR GREATNESS!
> — TAMIKA CATCHINGS
> WNBA EXECUTIVE

TAMIKA CATCHINGS
WNBA, 2002-2016

> Freedom means freedom of conscience and belief but it also includes the responsibility to make informed choices as citizens by voting and by obeying duly adopted laws and regulations.
> Sandra Day O'Connor

SANDRA DAY O'CONNOR
Supreme Court Justice 1981-2006

> FREEDOM ... is many things worth fighting for and dying for but for me, true freedom would be lying in a hammock on a Saturday afternoon with absolutely nothing to worry about.
> Mike McCurry
> W.H. Press Secretary, 1995-98

MIKE MCCURRY
White House Press Secretary 1995-1998

THE FREEDOM CARDS

SISTER ELAINE ROULET
Activist and Nun, d.2020

SISTER JEANNINE GRAMICK
LGBTQ Activist and Nun

SISTER HELEN PREJEAN
Activist and Nun

SISTER SIMONE CAMPBELL
Activist and Nun

Front   Back

ELIZABETH MCALISTER
Activist and Former Nun

> Freedom means that I have the freedom to do the Right things according to God's laws

SISTER THERESE BUI

Nun, Sisters of Carmelite, Salt Lake City, Utah

I knocked on the door of the Sisters of Carmelite unannounced. They welcomed me into a room with bars like a jail—Sister Bui on one side and me on the other.

"In the Heart of the Church, My Mother, I Shall Be Love"
(St. Therese of the Child Jesus)

CARMELITE MONASTERY
5714 Holladay Blvd
Salt Lake City, UT 84121

Freedom for all does not necessarily include justice or equality for all. So when we come into this world with unequal brains or environments or opportunities, it is incumbent upon a government to do the best job it can in overcoming those handicaps. There are those who will decry government for crimping their style. I say fie on them and to fight for that kind of government to provide that level playing field where all can thrive. For those who still rise to the top and become movers and shakers I say hooray and continue the fight for others' freedom to enjoy justice and equality.

ED ASNER

Actor

THE FREEDOM CARDS

FOX NEWS

1211 Avenue of the Americas
New York, New York 10036

Geraldo Rivera
Host

FREEDOM IS THE RIGHT TO WORSHIP (OR NOT) AS I PLEASE — TO LIVE AND WORK WHERE AND WHEN I CHOOSE — TO SELECT MY LEADERS — MY PERSONAL STYLE — MY LEISURE PURSUITS — CLOTHING — BASEBALL TEAM — CAR — TOOTHPASTE — BOOKS — MUSIC AND TV SHOWS. TO BREATHE THE FREE AIR OF OUR GREAT COUNTRY IS MY RIGHT AND PRIVILEGE AS A CITIZEN OF THE WORLD AND HISTORY'S GREATEST COUNTRY.

XXX Best wishes!
Geraldo

A NEWS CORPORATION COMPANY

GERALDO RIVERA
Journalist and TV Show Host

Protestors and Chicago police officers in Grant Park during the 1968 Democratic Convention

National Archives photo no. 6210767

THE FREEDOM CARDS

Freedom is the ability to do "good trouble"

John Froines
Chicago 7 and Professor/Activist

JOHN FROINES

Activist & Member of the Chicago 7

THE FREEDOM CARDS

"FREEDOM IS WORSHIPING GOD AND ENJOYING THE LIFE HE HAS BLESSED US WITH."

Mark Henn
ANIMATOR/DIRECTOR
WALT DISNEY STUDIOS

MARK HENN
Director and Animator

Freedom is ~~having this making yourse~~ being able to make mistakes.

Pete Docter
Director of Disney/Pixar's "Monsters, Inc." and "UP"

PETE DOCTER
Director

THE FREEDOM CARDS

> Liberty is the foundation stone of all human rights
>
> *Boutros Boutros-Ghali, Paris, August 2014*

BOUTROS BOUTROS-GHALI
UN Secretary General 1992-1996, d.2016

> FREEDOM'S JUST ANOTHER WORD FOR... NOTHIN' LEFT TO LOSE.
> (YOU CAN QUOTE ME ON THAT!)
> — WEIRD AL Yankovic

AL YANKOVIC
Singer-Songwriter

> Freedom stands tall, walks with dignity, love and grace for all who breathe life with dreams being fulfilled.
>
> *Odessa Cleveland, Actress, Artist, Author, Poet*

ODESSA CLEVELAND
Actress and Poet

> Freedom Obliges Me To Secure Freedom For Others!
>
> *Miep Gies, July 20, 2007. Anne Frank's friend and helper safeguarding once her diary.*

MIEP GIES
Protector of Anne Frank, d.2010

> Freedom is respecting yourself for who you are and knowing that life is worth living!
>
> *Dave Pallone, Author & National League Baseball Umpire*

DAVID PALLONE
Major League Umpire 1979-1988

> Freedom is enough detachment from my own self that I can seek the good of others and of society.
>
> *Fr. Richard Rohr, Franciscan author*

FATHER RICHARD ROHR
Franciscan Author

> "Freedom is the ability to reach for the stars. If you reach for the stars you may land on the roof. Reach for the roof? you may get to the clouds."
>
> *Tovah Feldshuh*

TOVAH FELDSHUH
Actress

> Freedom is the liberty to do whatever you desire without infringing upon another person.
>
> *Ammon Bundy — A free man :)*

AMMON BUNDY
Activist

THE FREEDOM CARDS

Confederate Flag Supporter

Rally in Support of the Confederate Flag, Stone Mountain Park, Georgia

August 1, 2015

Can I just be honest with you for a minute? I didn't know if I should have included these two pages. When I went to this rally, I spent time with the counter-protestors and then ventured into a packed parking lot of people all waving the confederate battle flag. I see a lot less of that flag now, especially after the Emanuel AME shooting. I decided to include this event because this was real. I was there.

THE FREEDOM CARDS

Members of the III% Security Force Militia complete cards, Stone Mountain Park, August 1, 2015. I saw General Blood Agent recently on the Showtime program *The Circus*, saying he would overturn the results of the 2020 election if Donald Trump lost.

> What freedom means to me? It means as long as I'm abiding by just laws I should be able to do and celebrate whatever I want

ANONYMOUS

> Your rights end when they infringe on mine.
>
> General Blood Agent
> Georgia Security Force III
> Commanding Officer

GENERAL BLOOD AGENT
Head of the Georgia III%ers

> Freedom means that The Constitution will not be infridged apon that we Have our freedoms because of the BRAVE Men and Woman that Risk there lives for us to protect our freedom
>
> John Gills
>
> American Citizen

JOHN GILLS

205

THE FREEDOM CARDS

> Freedom is the ability to exercise from one's innermost being, independence of thought, word and deed, to live courageously, to enable others to liberate themselves from fear, and in doing so to celebrate daily the ultimate triumph of one's spirit merging into one world.
> — Dennis J. Kucinich, US Congressman, World Citizen

DENNIS KUCINICH
Representative from Ohio's 10th 1997-2013

MORT WALKER
Cartoonist

> Freedom is the power to make informed choices from a set of opportunities that is wide enough to include more than one good option.
> — Daniel C. Dennett

DANIEL DENNETT
Philosopher and Author

> I AM A GREAT BELIEVER IN FREEDOM, AS LONG AS WE DON'T OVER THE BRINK INTO THE CATEGORY OF LACK OF DISCIPLINE. WHICH WE ARE DOING.
> — Gary Player

GARY PLAYER
Professional Golfer

> True freedom is to live without fear.
> — Lincoln Peirce, cartoonist

LINCOLN PEIRCE
Author, *Big Nate*

> Freedom, life's seed. All rights sprout from freedom.

BOB MARTINEZ
Governor of Florida 1987-1991

> Freedom is the to resist the empire — to not pay for it — to be willing to take the consequences —

FRANCES CROWE
Peace Activist, d.2018

> Freedom is our inheritance from our forefathers; we should treasure it & protect it.
> — Rich Lowry, Editor, National Review

RICH LOWRY
Editor of *National Review*

206

THE FREEDOM CARDS

HERMANN SCHEIPERS
German Catholic Priest Who Was Imprisoned at Dachau Concentration Camp between 1941 and 1945. d.2016

"Freedom is given where no one is prevented from expressing his or her opinion."

MARTE SKAARA
Norwegian Activist and Creator of The Climate Cards

JOHN DOUGLAS
Former FBI Agent and Early Criminologist

HAROLD BROWN
Secretary of Defense 1977-1981, d.2019

CHUCK YEAGER
Air Force General and Test Pilot, d.2020

207

THE FREEDOM CARDS

Base of the Washington Monument, The Inauguration of Donald Trump, Washington, D.C.

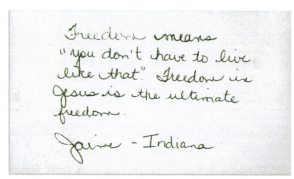

> Freedom means "you don't have to live like that". Freedom in Jesus is the ultimate freedom.
>
> Jaime – Indiana

JAIME

> Freedom gives us rights to believe in how we want as individuals. We can express our thoughts as we see even if others disagree.
>
> Dale A. Brown
> Dale A. Brown
> Retired –
> Brazil, IN

DALE

> Freedom means to me that Abaerham Linkin freed us. Freedom means that we are free and we aren't slaves
> Isabella. B. age 9

ISABELLA

208

THE FREEDOM CARDS

Donald Trump's Inauguration

January 17 to 21, 2017

> Means that our government follows the constitution as currently written & we the people keep it in check.
>
> Travis Jones

TRAVIS JONES

> Freedom is the opportunity to meet and build a friendships with people like you both. People that I can share experiences with and learn from.
>
> Ed Pitochelli
> Vernon, Connecticut

ED PITOCHELLI

> Living a free life with no restrictions or less restrictions.
>
> FRANK PAOLANTONIO

FRANK PAOLANTONIO

> CHOICES
>
> Lauren McFerin Johnson
>
> AN AMERICAN

LAUREN JOHNSON

> To be able to change the world without restrictions
>
> Liam D. McFernin
>
> Student, Invisioner, age 12

LIAM MCFERNIN

> Freedom IS
>
> Susana Martinez
> NM Governor

SUSANA MARTINEZ
Governor of New Mexico (2011-2019)

> FREEDOM IS THE WISDOM TO KNOW WHAT A PRIVILEGE IT IS TO BE AN AMERICAN, TO UNDERSTAND WHAT THAT MEANS AND THE AMOUNT OF PRIDE THAT COMES WITH IT.
>
> CHARLES A. FRANCO
>
> FIRST GENTLEMAN FOR THE STATE OF NEW MEXICO

CHARLES FRANCO
First Gentleman of New Mexico

THE FREEDOM CARDS

> being free to live and act without ~~upper~~ constraints
>
> Margaret Ruttman
> librarian and former teacher

MARGARET RUTTMAN
Hansford County Library, Spearman, Texas

> Freedom means that we have the right to make choices. We can choose to make good decisions and do the right thing.
>
> Cathy McMaster
> Arnettsville Public Library Librarian

CATHY MCMASTER
Arnettsville Public Library, Morgantown, West Virginia

Arnettsville Public Library, Morgantown, West Virginia

> Freedom is the ability follow your dreams and accomplish the things that are important to you.
> Virginia Grossen
> McCoy Public Library Director

VIRGINIA GROSSEN
McCoy Public Library, Shullsburg, Wisconsin

> Freedom to me is the inalienable right to question.
> Janice Grace
> Mom
> G-mom
> Mgr. Local History Room
> Citizen

JANICE GRACE
Long Branch Free Public Library, Long Branch, New Jersey

210

THE FREEDOM CARDS

> To be free to choose, to be responsible for one's choices. To live w/out fear.
> GOOD QUESTION!
>
> Sharon Crotser-Toy
> SHARON CROTSER-TOY

SHARON CROTSER-TOY
Watervliet District Library, Lawrence, Michigan

> To me freedom is personal, meaning I am in charge of writing the chapters in my own book of life.
>
> Heather Kinkade
>
> I am a librarian at Brigham Memorial Library in Sharon, Wisconsin.

HEATHER KINKADE
Waterford Public Library, Waterford, Wisconsin

Arnettsville Public Library, Morgantown, West Virginia

> Freedom is being able to Read whatever I want to Read.
>
> Michele Timmons
> Library Director

MICHELE TIMMONS
Elgin City Public Library, Elgin, Oregon

Librarians I met when driving across America.

The Freedom Road Trip
Summer 2017

211

THE FREEDOM CARDS

> Where any child can be or do whatever they want.

CHUCK TODD
Journalist

> Freedom to me is the ability to surrender my life to Jesus Christ and to be able to rest freely in His ability to give purpose to my life
> Susan Raye
> entertainer

SUSAN RAYE
Country Music Singer

> Freedom is the ability to have a dream and the liberty to attain it.

MICHAEL PENA
Actor

> Freedom can only be fully achieved when no human being, and no part of humanity, is subordinated to and exploited by another. In the largest sense, freedom means human beings as a whole applying a scientifically-grounded approach in order to continually recognize and overcome obstacles to dealing with each other and with the rest of nature, in a positively beneficial way, to develop an economy, institutions, and relations among people based on cooperation, not exploitation and oppression, and to provide for the flourishing of individuals within that overall cooperative and mutually beneficial framework.
> Bob Avakian, author of The New Communism

BOB AVAKIAN
Leader of the Revolutionary Communist Party, USA

> To me freedom means being able to express yourself in a respectful way. Having the freedom to live and follow your dreams.
> Carla Overbeck
> USA Soccer

CARLA OVERBECK
Team USA Soccer 1988-2000

> Freedom gives each of us the ability to pursue our dreams, our goals and our passions as we see fit - freedom is the key to happiness.

CHRIS CHRISTIE
Governor of New Jersey 2010-2018

> Freedom means "unbounded" Possibilities - think, reach, achieve!
> Tom Franks

TOMMY FRANKS
General, United States Army

> Freedom is having the opportunity to be whatever you want to be in life and making it happen.
> Leroy Kelly
> #44 H.O.F 94

LEROY KELLY
NFL Player

THE FREEDOM CARDS

> It means I can realize any dream and do anything in pursuit of that dream!
> — Michael Steele

MICHAEL STEELE
Chairman of the Republican National Committee 2009-2011

> The freedom = democration; the rights to choose
> — Václav Nedomanský

VÁCLAV NEDOMANSKÝ
Czech Hockey Player Who Defected to North America in 1974 to Play Hockey

> Freedom means being a responsible citizen... learning about the expectations of living in a democracy... having your own beliefs and opinions, not influenced or forced on you by others.
> — Glenn Close

GLENN CLOSE
Actress

> Freedom is a very precious treasure to be cherished, protected and respected. Let us make sure that the United States of America, will always be our great and beautiful country, and the image of liberty and democracy.
> — Magda Herzberger
> A Holocaust Survivor of three death camps Auschwitz-Birkenau, Bremen and Bergen Belsen
> February 27, 2013

MAGDA HERZBERGER
Holocaust Survivor, d.2021

> Freedom is the minimization of rules and maximization of opportunity.
> — Andy Weir

ANDY WEIR
Writer

> Freedom means you can do any experiment you want, not only in science but in life. It's a very successful idea, and a pleasant one too.
> — Frank Wilczek

FRANK WILCZEK
Nobel Prize in Physics in 2004

> American freedom is not just the freedom to do what you want to do, but the freedom to do what you ought to do. That is why we are a great nation.
> — Rick Santorum

RICK SANTORUM
Senator from Pennsylvania 1995-2007

> Freedom to me means the right to think what I want to think and say what I want to say.
> — Bob Schieffer
> CBS News Chief Washington Correspondent

BOB SCHIEFFER
Journalist

THE FREEDOM CARDS

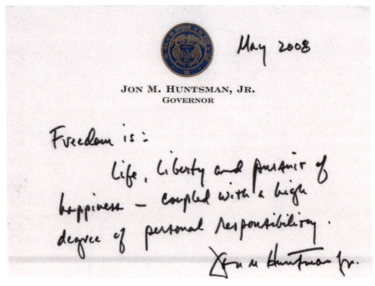

JON HUNTSMAN

Governor of Utah 2005-2009, Ambassador to China
2009-2001, Ambassador to Russia 2017-2019

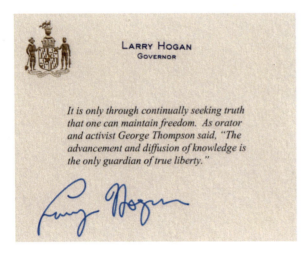

LARRY HOGAN

Governor of Maryland District 2015-

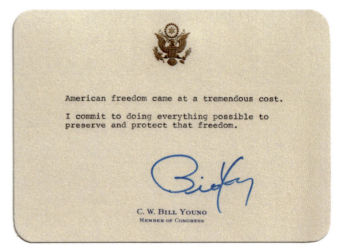

BILL YOUNG

Representative from Florida 1971-2013, d.2013

THE FREEDOM CARDS

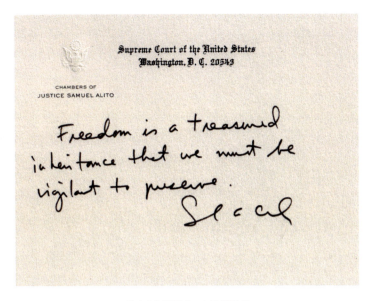

SAMUEL ALITO

Supreme Court Justice

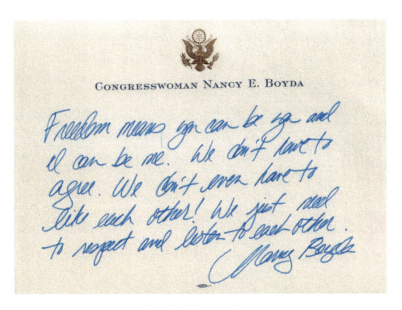

NANCY BOYDA

Representative from Kansas's 2nd 2007-2009

Me collecting Freedom Cards, Joe Biden South Carolina Victory Rally, Columbia, SC. Photo by Francis Millar Dayrit.

The South Carolina Democratic Primary
in 2020 was held on a leap day.

Washington, May 29, 2013

Washington

Gabriella Augustsson

Dear Mr. Robson:

While our ambassador found your project on the meaning of freedom to various people around the world to be ambitious, he has chosen to express his freedom to not participate in your survey.

Sincerely,

Gabriella Augustsson
Counselor, Public Affairs and Diplomacy

Postal Address:
2900 K Street, NW
Washington, DC 20007

Visitors' address:
901 30th Street, NW
Washington, DC 20007

Telephone:
(202) 467-2600
Fax:
(202) 467-2699

E-mail:
ambassaden.washington@gov.se
Web site:
www.swedenabroad.com/washington

MASSACHUSETTS INSTITUTE OF TECHNOLOGY

Department of Linguistics and Philosophy
77 Massachusetts Avenue, 32-D808
Cambridge, Massachusetts 02139

November 27, 2006

Dear Alex Robson,

I've thought about your request, but can't fulfill it I'm afraid. I don't see how to say anything sensible about a notion as important as freedom in a space shorter than a serious essay.

Sincerely,

Noam Chomsky

THE FREEDOM CARDS

My name is Louise Pryor. We receive mail addressed to Senator David Pryor a lot. In fact my husband was David Pryor just not the Senator. I will tell you what Freedom means to me. My husband served his country in Vietnam 1967-1968. He passed away last month of cancer from Agent Orange

Front

exposure. So in a way he gave his life for his country. Freedom is never free. It comes at a cost. Thank god there are men like my husband who were willing to pay the Price.

Thank you
Louise Pryor

LOUISE PRYOR

Back

THE FREEDOM CARDS

46°37'51.2"N 98°47'50.7"W
ND-46
Jud, North Dakota

Photo taken during The Freedom Road Trip

Whenever you are on the road in North Dakota, that is straight, warm, and sun battered, and you haven't seen anyone or anything besides the deserted shacks that were built for the farmhands who once picked the crops every fall, you will feel far from everything. You will feel far from the Rocky Mountains that were once crossed by the settlers. You will feel far from the East Coast beaches that have sands that move every moment to the beat of the waves. You will feel far from the oil rigs of Texas, and the tall cold buildings of Chicago, Oregon's rocky coast, sailboats off Tybee Island, one-screen movie theaters in Nebraska, and the Mississippi River that flows deeply to the gulf. You will feel far from your family, from your friends, and your home. You will feel like the road will stretch forever without turning, and there are no living things except you and the giant, winged birds that glide above.

But eventually, a fellow traveler will appear as a dot coming from the west. As you draw closer, the tractor's big back tires will clear, and the driver will be looking down the road just as you are. You'll get closer and closer until you are about to pass, and his hand will wave, not because he has mistaken you for his brother or a friend he once knew, but because you are both travelers on the same road. Every bit of suffering and struggle—from the Continental Army at Valley Forge, the civil rights protesters on the Edmund Pettus Bridge, families on the Oregon Trail, children who once labored in squalid factories, Harriet Tubman, who guided slaves to freedom, uncounted millions who passed through Ellis Island, and millions more who now clumsily and imperfectly try to make a life that resembles that of the American Dream—has come together in the single tip of the farmer's finger. The valleys and hills of his callused hand mirror perfectly those of the Appalachian foothills. His wrinkles show the same pathways of the tributaries of the Ohio River. He—like you and me—are brothers and sisters of freedom. American Freedom—imperfect yet declared as perfect. We hold it in our skin, and tongues, and hands; the same hands that grip onto a country whose promises are not yet fulfilled.

If you would like to add your voice to The Freedom Cards,
please send your card answering the question,
"What does freedom mean to you?" to:

The Freedom Cards
c/o Alex Robson
PO Box 98133
Atlanta, GA 30359

Transcriptions of Selected Cards

Page 4
Howard Kakita: Freedom is being able to share our devastating experiences to mitigate future generations from experiencing a similar plight.

Page 10
Deborah Taylor: Freedom is the ability to hope, dream, and pursue life's challenges. Finding the rewards of one's own mind and hands to build a future for yourself and family.

Annette Rath: Means choices—my right choices—Plans + rights – Peace of mind

Juanita Ott: Freedom means everyone has the right to pursue their talents and interest regardless of income or family background. It also means that rights of the minority are not overpowered by the majority.

Linda Beatty: Freedom is living without fear of physical, mental, or social dangers from the government based on sex, race, or one's beliefs.

Page 14
Nishanth Sidduri: A woman's right to choose free from intimidation, retribution or fear of unjust consequence.

Page 21
Uriah Fields: Freedom means choosing myself and doing as I please in light of taking responsibility for my decisions.

Kathleen Cleaver: The legal guarantee and presence of social custom to exercise your right to life, health, opportunities for education, access to meaningful employment, ability to protect your property, your family, and pursue your goals in life without obstacles based on racial or sexual status, religion or immigration status.

Page 24
Marty Walsh: Freedom is to dream big, and follow that dream no matter what.

Nancy Chamberland: Freedom is the absence of fear and the ability to enjoy equality, pride, mutual acceptance, right to work...all the dreams of our brave living and dead.

Page 28
Frank Pommersheim: Freedom is the joy to find friendship in this world w/whomever we please.

Nikki Giovanni: Freedom: the responsibility to acknowledge and embrace the truth; the obligation to expose the lies of governmental, religious and cultural bigots.

Page 29
Jerry Linenger: The Foundation of innovation & inspiration. Allowing us to dream big! To reach for the stars. To have no limits!!!

Larry King: Freedom is the Bill of Rights especially the first amendment.

Page 35
Walter Ehlers: Freedom means love for God and Country. The American Flag of the United State means freedom to more people than any other symbol in our World.

Page 37
Paul Bucha: Within each person resides the potential to challenge destiny, waiting only for that important time when events and circumstances so combine—FREEDOM allows each of us to find that potential and throughly change the world.

Nick Bacon: To me Freedom is the opportunity for my children to live a life in a country that allows them the individual pursuit of education, prosperity and joy. Mainly Freedom gives me and my family the privilege of worshiping God as free Christians.

James Taylor: I enjoy freedom because Americans before me were willing to sacrifice their lives to establish, protect and preserve it for me. I am privileged. It is now my responsibility to protect and preserve Freedom, as we know it today, for future generations.

Page 39
Charles Murray: Freedom should be cherished by all Americans. We should never forget that it has been given to us by others—by others who suffered, bled and died on battlefields, in the air and on the seas around the world—by others who held their nation and their comrades above themselves—by others who continue to serve for us so that we may live in freedom.

Thomas Hudner: Freedom is the privilege to speak, pray, and live one's life as he wishes but without encroaching on others. We have the responsibility to act in any way necessary to preserve this blessing passed down to us through great wisdom, courage, sacrifice and honor.

Ola Mize: You have never lived until you have almost died—for those who fought for "freedom," life has a "special flavor" the protected will never know.

Harold Fritz: Freedom is the basic building block that provides equality for each of its recipients. Country of origin, race or ethnic background are not limitations for one to enjoy Freedom. Freedom is a very fragile element to be guarded closely and protected.

Francis Curry: There are so many freedoms in this country (to travel, religion, speech, etc.) denied in other countries that one does not enhance or diminish the others.

Page 41
Allen Lynch: To me Freedom is the ability to choose how to live, worship, vote and to be all I can be by the Grace of God.

Robert Ingram: Our freedom was fought for, died for by our forefathers who wrote our Constitution to protect us and our freedom. Today our freedoms are being threatened from many directions. Our rights as laid out in the Constitution are being overturned by radicals and other Leftists: Religion, the 2nd Amendment right to bear arms, and many others.
    I have faith that you and your generation will overcome and protect our Constitution proudly.

Page 44
Frederick Blesse: —Freedom—
1. Freedom to me is to have the option to choose one's direction in life and then pursue it to the utmost of your ability.
2. Cherish your failures. If you are smart, you will learn the most from them.

John Walker: Freedom is the ability to live your own life as you wish and allowing others to do so too.

Page 49
Michael Hayden: Freedom is the right to fully live your human potential.

THE FREEDOM CARDS

Page 53
Ethan Gordon: A land of freedom is a land where chance alone does not determine one's lot in life. Even in the worst of times, America always has potential to be the land of the free, and we should all help it get there.

Glenda Chen: Music, when done with heart, when shared with the right group of people, gives me freedom. So I'd have to say that freedom is whatever circumstances give me the ability to feel that spark of enlightenment and joy—it's a freedom that resonates with others and radiates beyond just myself.

Page 61
Protestor 1: Then end of fascism and neoliberalism social, racial, and environmental justice

Protestor 2: The autonomous institution of society before that society's institutionalization.

Page 67
Bernard Dakymgele: Freedom is the best thing in the world and the USA is the best thing that happened to the world.

Page 70
Kirsten Gillibrand: Freedom is the essence of our democracy–freedom of speech, freedom to vote, freedom to live our lives and provide for our children so they may achieve their God-given potential.

Page 71
Sandra Fluke: Freedom is an essential, but insufficient ingredient in full equality. We must work to ensure our citizens also have the means to effectuate their dreams and do not face inequitable barriers.

Sheldon Harnick: In America, thank Heaven we are free to express our opinions, politically and every other way, and although we may invite problems from those who disagree with us, at least our Government may not interfere with the expression of those opinions!

Phyllis Coates: Freedom to me means no radicals in my country—we people obeying our laws and loving the USA.

Page 72
Rudy Boschwitz: Freedom means "Magnificent America." I arrived in the U.S. at 5 in 1935 from Germany. Of my family that started behind, one survived WWII. So, "Magnificent America" means life and freedom. To the work "Magnificent American" means peace. The 68 years since WWII is the longest period of peace without war between major powers in history.

Page 84
Herschel Walker: Freedom is having the right to have your own thought. To dream and run for that dream.

Page 87
Mike Ditka: Grateful being able to live in the USA and make choices.

Don Zimmer: I chose baseball as my career. No one told me or said I had to. That is the tip of the iceberg of what freedom is. "Freedom of choice!?!"

Page 90
Randy Newman: The freedom afforded the individual in this country at least in regard to freedom of expression has allowed me to write about anything I want without having to worry about prison. I've taken full advantage of the freedom we have here and I'm very grateful for it.

Stephen Breyer: Freedom under the Constitution means two very different things. The first - a very ancient liberty - is the freedom to take part in government. That's called democracy. The second - a more modern liberty - the freedom to lead our lives free of government control - for example freedom of speech. If our government is to work both kinds of freedom are necessary: an active participation in civic life and protection against tyranny - even by the majority.

Page 91
Gloria Steinem: I wish so much that I could agree with your theme "Every American has one thing in common…freedom" Freedom means being part of nature, and killing pollution too often comes between us and even air and water.

Freedom means the power to choose, but young people now graduate with such huge debt—just to get the education given freely in other prosperous countries—that they must often enter into jobs they wouldn't otherwise choose. Freedom means governance of one's own body, but the current U.S. government tries to deprive women that—here and in other countries.

So I cherish relative freedom and use it to gain true freedom—and a world in which everyone matters.

Grover Norquist: Freedom means you and I are free to live and lead our own lives. You may not steal from others and they as individuals or through any gang or covenant may not steal your prosperity, your income, your life or your future.Everyone keeps their hands to themselves. No hitting. Hugging allowed. Freedom is life. Limits on freedom are limits on life.

Page 94
Lou Holtz: To me, freedom means you are responsible for your success, happiness and your future. You cannot remain free if you hold the Government or others responsible for your success, failure, or happiness.

Margaret Keane: Freedom means to me to be "set free from enslavement to corruption and have the glorious freedom of the children of God" promised at Roman 8:21 and then having freedom to live forever on a paradise "earth". PS 37:29.

Page 95
Edward Albee: Freedom from: oppression, from want, from discrimination, from video surveillance. Freedom to: be-within moral and legal barriers-live as I please, with whom I please, and allowed to express myself freely.

Jeremiah Wright: Freedom means accepting and embracing all human beings as equals who are made in the image of God: and who have a right to quality education, health care and a living wage.

Page 108
James Leavelle: Freedom to me means: I can go where I please when I please. I can worship where I choose and, best of all, I can visit my friends and family any time I choose.

Ronald Jones: Freedom allows one to be educated, and be employed, have their own religious beliefs, vote in elections, travel out of their own country, own property, have children, and have freedom of speech.

Page 109
Cyril Wecht: Freedom in a true democracy is a guarantee that you will not be persecuted or prosecuted because of your race, religion, ethnicity, or political beliefs, Freedom includes and assures the right to be physically safe from unfettered police misconduct and to have civil and criminal justice systems that function fairly and objectively.

Page 115
Carolyn Maloney: Freedom is the right to think, act, speak as your conscious dictates and equal opptortunity for all!

Nigel Farage: Independent UK

Page 117
James Watson: Freedom to me is the ability to think about and say and write to others what I believe to be reality. (the truth).

Diane Watson: Freedom means having choices and options to live my life without fear of what I might say or think as long as I do not go over legal lines!

Oliver North: Freedom is the right to pray as we want, come and go as we wish, speak as we please—and use our God-given gifts and talents as we desire.

Ann Northrop: Freedom is the fundamental cornerstone of a life of value. But it is an empty promise without a guarantee of food and shelter and health. The human race must respect all its members before it can claim to confer "freedom" for all.

Charles Albury: Freedom is something that is God given. It doesn't come easy. Too many Americans don't realize all the death our countrymen gave so we could have Freedom today. God Bless them all.

Nikki Haley: Freedom is to live in a country where you can be successful as you want to be and nothing will get in your way.

Page 127
Hans-Jochen Vogel : For Me, freedom means leading a self-determined life that is based on the basic values of human dignity, justice, and solidarity.

Jerry Jeff Walker: As a young man I hitchhiked all over this country. I used to say I was America's guest. I street sang and wound up playing in the White House. Thanks to freedom I had a great ride.

Fred Johnson: A good garden provides room to grow, air, sunshine, and fertility. All these things work in harmony to enable plants to achieve their full potential. Freedom does the same for mankind.

Page 128
Gene Robinson: For me, freedom is the ability and blessing to choose my path in the direction I discern God's calling to me, while maintaining my love for (and responsibility to) my neighbor.

Mary Costa: Freedom is being able to express that nothing is more important to me than my walk with God.

Page 130
Art Donovan: I served for "freedom."

Benjamin Ferencz: Freedom is the right to alter entrenched ideas by working for a world order governed by law rather than war.

Leon Panetta: Strengthen our freedoms and you strengthen our democracy—weaken our freedom and you weaken our democracy.

Page 131
Ben Kuroki: Freedom is the blessing that inspired me to fight like hell for the right to fight for my country.

Joan Berger: Freedom to me meant I could become a professional woman baseball player and travel the country.

Page 132
James Schlesinger: Freedom means two interlocking elements:
The individual, family or group are free from the coercive power of the State.
With that freedom, each may pursue-and should pursue-his/her appreciation for the well-being of society.

Page 133
Henry Kissinger: Freedom is the ability to live your hopes

Page 138
Tina Louise: Freedom to me means loving who I want, reading what I want, expressing my opinions as I please, living in a Democracy and praying that it will bring peace soon.

Page 139
Aníbal Acevedo Vilá: Freedom is love because we are freest when we are with those we love most. To affirm humanity's right to freedom is to affirm our love for humanity and life itself.

Joan Rivers: Freedom is the right to believe as I wish, to live as I wish, and to express how I feel without anyone imposing their thoughts on me.

Art Laffer: Economics is all about incentives. And freedom assures that incentives are aligned with the good of all.

Page 156
Jason Alexander: Freedom is the ultimate gift and expression of our humanity for each other. It is how we say- "I believe in you, I trust you and I wish you a good and fulfilling life." Freedom is the greatest show of respect was can offer another person.

Page 158
Gary Busey: Freedom gives you the ability to chase and catch your dreams and if you don't have that freedom, your imagination will live in "empty spaces." God bless your freedom which comes from being an American.

Silas Hathaway: My wife Shirley then freedom is the most important thing I have. Every morning tying my shoe laces I am reminded of my WWII service as a tank commander in Rabat North Africa—only a thumb for a left hand on Mar 3rd.

Page 160
Andrew Quinn: Freedom is having the means to control the way you want to live, the ability to pursue the lifestyle and goals you want to live, and to be responsible and accountable for outcomes you achieve.

Page 161
David Ellison: Freedom is the right to be an independent person who respects the rights of others, free to love God and be witness in speech and actions.

Page 163
Paul Berg: Freedom empowers us to seek and achieve one's dreams and ambitions. Being free also provides us with an irrevocable right to question, seek answers and to publicize the findings of the investigations.

Michael Brown: To me, freedom is the right to be wrong. It is the right to be in the minority and to still enjoy the same liberties as those in the majority.

Charles Townes: Freedom encourages creativity, allowing individuals to break with standardized thought and behavior.

Henry Heimlich: Freedom will come about when we become a caring world. A caring world will come about when we stop the stupidity and end wars. When the money spent on wars is used to provide all people with food, health care, and a safe environment, we will have a caring world and be free.

Page 166
Jessica Curley: I am my own and make my own decisions.

Cindy Curley: Freedom to me is the right of everyone to pursue love, peace, the pursuit to live, work, receive an education, without interruption or hate or discrimination.

Page 168
Eddie Robinson: Freedom to me is to be able to think, do, and say anything I want as long as I stay within the law.

Page 169
Robert Ballard: Freedom means no one is taking care of you.

Edgar Wayburn: Freedom is something we all want but, surprisingly, seldom have.

Holly Near: Freedom is complex and personal. Do I stand with the singer or the censor? The rapist or the raped? And at what risk? My daily choices introduce me to freedom—and to myself.

Page 173
John McCain: The service of every past and present American soldier has helped guarantee the freedom we enjoy today.

Michael Dukakis: Freedom to me means the ability to be deeply and actively involved in politics and public service in my community and in my country without fear or favor.

Bob Dole: Freedom is responsibility. It is living our lives the way we choose while respecting the rights of others to do the same, and who do the same for us. While it is rooted in basic laws, it is more importantly anchored in a tradition of responsibility, mutual respect and duty that must accompany freedom in order for it to thrive. When expressed appropriately, and defended from threat or coercion or malice, freedom is the principle that elevates humanity and allows us to fulfill our tremendous promise. It does not guarantee individual results, but it provides the only foundation upon which they can possibly be achieved.

Sarah Palin: Freedom is what the human spirit longs for! It's one of the few things in life that's worth both living and dying for–as our brave women and men in uniform know.

Page 177
James Risen: Freedom is the right to do and say whatever I wish, unfettered by an onerous government or corrupt private interests.

Page 179
Manuela Well-Off-Man: Freedom means to be able to exhibit challenging, thought provoking, cutting edge art, and to give artists, who are often overlooked by the mainstream art world, a voice.

Page 180
Desmond Tutu: It means being free to be human.

Page 181
Belly Williams: Freedom for me is the love of Mother Earth. Freedom for me is working to set others free. Freedom for me is knowing that each person I educate in the techniques of non-violence will educate others, and then one day war will be obsolete! That's freedom for me!

David Trimble: An open society and the rule of law are essential for any county that aspires to be prosperous and free. I am content to rely on the freedom we have built up, step by step through the common law and the British empirical tradition, capable of modification and change through our flexible "constitution."

THE FREEDOM CARDS

Page 182:
Fats Domino: Freedom to me is to be able to say whatever you would like to, with truthful meaning and not cause harm to anyone and please keep God in mind.

Steven Schwartz: Freedom is the ability to make one's own choices, right or wrong, as long as they don't hurt others.

Page 183:
George Shearing: Freedom is having the privilege of playing concerts for people without being afraid–where everyone can truly enjoy themselves both onstage and off.

Page 184:
Erwin Schild: Freedom means to have the choice to participate in society: to lead, to devote, or to withdraw and be left alone. Freedom is contingent on everyone else enjoying the same opportunities. The individual is free only in a free society governed by rules that protect, enhance and promote freedom for all.
    Growing up in Nazi Germany, I experienced the very opposite of freedom and learned to treasure life in a free society and to stand on guard for freedom.

William Ayers: Freedom—the act of naming the obstacles to our full humanity and then joining hands to breach those barriers—relies on imagination, that "slow fuse of possibility," to illuminate a world that could be or should be, but is not yet.

Tommy Chong: Freedom to me? Means— You can try and be anyone you want. And it's alright to fail…we have the freedom to fail and still play the game.

Page 185
Ken Jennings: "Freedom" is my favorite part of living in a liberal democracy but only my 3rd favorite Wham! single. ("Careless Whisper" and "Wham Rap!" are better IMHO.)

Joe Arpaio: Freedom is the world's greatest supernatural resource.

Bill Nye: For me, freedom is the ability to do what each of us wants to pursue happiness here on Earth; it highlights the opportunity for each of us to be responsible for our own actions and to leave the world better than we found it.

Page 186
Dutch VanKirk: Freedom is the right to make my choice of what to think and do.

Dakota Meyer: —Freedom is being an American! —Freedom is having the means to make your own decisions that decide your own Destiny! —Freedom is what we see every day we wake up. It's the view of what so many servicemen and women have sacrificed for!

S. Brian Wilson: Freedom is the ability to live actively and spontaneously without harming others or nature, deeply knowing that an injustice anywhere is a threat to justice everywhere. It takes corrective responsibility when harms from one's actions are made known.

Mary Blanchard Bowe: Freedom to me is being able to speak about what you want, do what you want, be what you want, eat what you want, live where you want, love and like who you want, study what you want, think what you want, feel what you want, go where you want, work where you want, have the religion you want with minimal individual restrictions.

Page 187
Archie Maltbie: Freedom is the most important human condition required for the fullest development. I fought in WWII as a fighter pilot for the freedom of my country, my family, myself and all the people of the world, including the people of my enemies.

THE FREEDOM CARDS

Page 191
John Harbaugh: Freedom is God's gracious gift that makes us His precious children. It is our responsibility to defend that gift always.

Page 194
Dennis Banks: The right to be who we were born, free to follow our own beliefs, our own spiritual path, our own language, songs and understandings! To believe in mother earth and our own creator.

Daniel Ellsberg: Freedom includes the right and the ability to say what you believe, to tell the truth, that others need to know, and even if it's "secret." (This may take courage.)

Karl Rove: Freedom means the right to chart a course for one's life, independent of the dictates of government, except for those limited rules necessary to protect the rights of others.

Colin McGinn: 1) Freedom is the ability to say to people what they don't want to hear. 2) Freedom is the ability to say what most people find repellent. 3) Freedom is toleration of the outrageous.

Page 195
Henry Rollins: Freedom allows you to call out the bad, the wrong, the awful–and perhaps change it. Freedom is why the Civil Rights Act of 1964 was signed into law, against the wishes of then Senator of Georgia Richard Russell. Russell had the freedom to be a bigot, like Marco Rubio. Freedom, real freedom that is—requires moral strength. Do you have it? Never stop asking.

Ron Paul: Freedom gives us peace and prosperity. It happens when the government is restrained.

Page 196
Elaine Roule: Freedom is being a woman in prison about to be released and finding in her cell telling her that the day she is reduced, a nun will be at the gate to bring her to a nice home and a new beginning.

Simone Campbell: Freedom is the fire of democracy—it warms the community and lights the path to a common good.

Elizabeth McAlister: Freedom—tune, resources, support…etc. It is not simple, one must have adequate financial resources to act freely. One must have a solid analysis on which to base one's actions. Ideally, one should have a circle of thoughtful people with whom to discern when, where, how to act concerning justice and peace. A prayerful circle is also central to right relations and right action, and the ability to evaluate each action in that circle is the best way for its members to grow into more and more thoughtful and peaceful action and conduct. No easy walk but so so valuable.

Page 198
Ed Asner: Freedom for all does not necessarily include justice or equality for all. So when we come into this world with unequal brains or environments or opportunities, it is incumbent upon a government to do the best job it can in overcoming those handicaps. There are those who will decry government for cramping their style. I say fie on them and to fight for that kind of government to provide that level playing field where all can thrive, and those who still rise to the top and become movers and shakers, I say hooray and continue the fight for others' freedom to enjoy justice and equality.

Page 203
Odessa Cleveland: Freedom stands tall, walks with dignity, love and grace for all who breathe life with dreams being fulfilled.

Richard Rohr: Freedom is enough detachment from my own self so that I can seek the good of others and of society.

Tovah Feldshuh: Freedom is the ability to reach for the stars. If you reach for the stars you may land on the roof. Reach for the roof. You may get off the ground.

Page 206
Dennis Kucinich: Freedom is the ability to exercise from one's innermost being, independence of thought, word, and deed; to live courageously, to enable others to liberate themselves from fear, and in doing so, to celebrate daily the ultimate triumph of one's spirit merging into one world.

Daniel Dennett: Freedom is the power to make informed choices from a set of opportunities that is wide enough to include more than one good option.

Frances Crowe: Freedom is to resist the empire—to not pay for it—to be willing to take the consequences.

Rich Lowry: Freedom is our inheritance from our forefathers; we should treasure it and protect it.

Page 207:
John Douglas: Freedom comes with a price. Without freedom our lives would be one of constant fear and chaos. Today we live in a world where our freedoms are challenged daily. Freedom is life—and life is worth fighting for.

Harold Brown: Freedom is the opportunity to use one's talents and abilities, inborn or acquired, to the fullest extent possible, consistent with the equal rights of others. It includes the right of philosophic and scientific inquiry, of expression of opinion and the exercise of religion, among other rights.

Chuck Yeager: I spent 50 years in Air Force Cockpits, fighting in 4 wars for my freedoms, and I enjoy the hell out of it!

Page 209
Charles Franco: Freedom is the wisdom to know what a privilege it is to be an American, to understand what that means and the amount of pride that comes with it.

Page 212
Bob Avakian: Freedom can only be fully achieved when no human being and no part of humanity is subordinated to and exploited by another. In the largest sense, freedom means human beings as a whole applying a scientifically grounded approach in order to continually recognize and overcome obstacles to deal with each other, and the rest of nature, in a financially beneficial way, to develop an economy, institutions, and relations, among people based on cooperation, not exploitation and oppression, and to provide for the flourishing of individuals with that overall cooperative and mutually beneficial framework.

Page 213
Václav Nedomanský: Freedom = Democracy, the right to choose.

Glenn Close: Freedom means being a responsible citizen…learning about the expectations of living in a democracy…having your own beliefs and options, not influenced or forced on you by others.

Magda Herzberger: Freedom is a very precious treasure to be cherished, protected and respected. Let us make sure that the United States of America, will always be our great and beautiful country, and the image of liberty and democracy.

Frank Wilczek: Freedom means you can do any experiment you want, not only in science but in life. It's a very successful idea, and a pleasant one too.